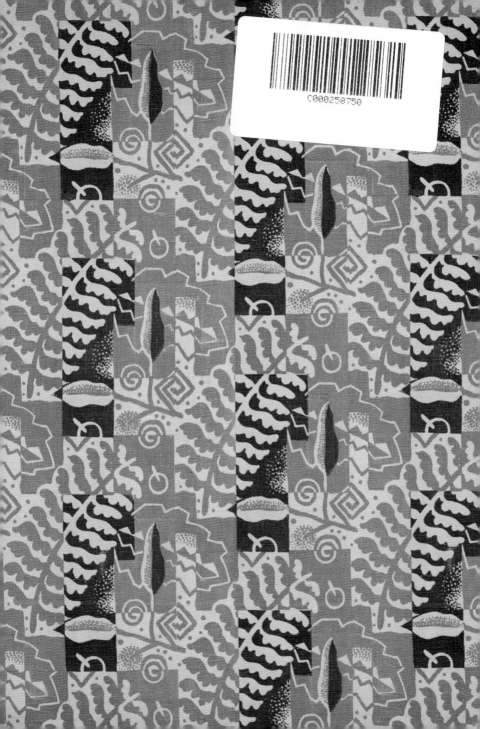

C000258750

GOOD FOOD ON
THE AGA

Persephone Book N° 45
Published by Persephone Books Ltd 2003

First published 1933 by Faber & Faber
© Faber & Faber

Endpapers taken from a 1933 block-printed linen
furnishing fabric designed by Bernard Adeney
for Allan Walton Textiles
© the Trustees of the Victoria & Albert Museum, London

Typeset in ITC Baskerville by Keystroke,
Jacaranda Lodge, Wolverhampton

Colour by Classic Cheney Press, Banbury

Printed and bound by Biddles Ltd,
Guildford and King's Lynn

ISBN 1 903155 355

Persephone Books Ltd
59 Lamb's Conduit Street
London WC1N 3NB
020 7242 9292

www.persephonebooks.co.uk

GOOD FOOD ON
THE AGA

by

AMBROSE HEATH

✳✳✳✳✳✳✳

illustrated

by

EDWARD BAWDEN

PERSEPHONE BOOKS
LONDON

ACKNOWLEDGEMENTS

THE author is indebted to Miss M. S. Frood, M.B.E., Warden of the Helena Club, London, who has been kind enough to allow him to use her recipes for fruit and jam bottling on the AGA Cooker.

A large part of the recipes in this book have appeared in the columns of *The Manchester Guardian*, *The Morning Post* and *The News-Chronicle*, and the author is indebted to the Editors of those newspapers for their permission to reprint the necessary extracts.

Many light-covered Cookery Books are impracticable for use in the kitchen. The Publishers of *Good Food on the Aga* desire to point out that the cover is both WATERPROOF and WASHABLE

FOREWORD

THE same good fortune which sent us voyaging some years ago to discover the AGA Cooker in Sweden has led us to Mr. Ambrose Heath, whose writings on gastronomical matters are already well known.

In writing this book for AGA, Mr. Heath has achieved far more than we ourselves visualised when the book was planned, for not only has he written on the best way of securing the greatest use and satisfaction from the cooker, but he tells of many dishes singularly fitted for preparation on it; dishes which are gathered from the cuisine of many lands and which will help to brighten our table.

In a recent book, Mr. Heath wrote: "Food that is worth eating cannot usually be flung together and dished up in a hurry and I have assumed that those who will like and use this book will be those who are ready to give some thought and care to the preparation of their meals."

It is therefore to those of our owners, and their Cooks, who appreciate good food, and the many exquisite ways in which it can be prepared, that this book is offered, in the sincere hope that, aided by the AGA and guided by the masterly hand of Mr. Ambrose Heath, they will achieve even greater culinary successes than ever before.

BELL'S HEAT APPLIANCES LTD.

Bestobell Works, Slough,
Buckinghamshire.

7

NOTE

The AGA Cooker was invented and patented by Dr. Gustaf Dalén, the Swedish Physicist and Nobel Prize Winner. It has been on the Swedish Market for many years and was first introduced into this country by Bell's Asbestos and Engineering Supplies Ltd., which was responsible for the formation of Bell's Heat Appliances Ltd. This latter Company now manufactures and markets the AGA cooker in Great Britain.

The AGA Cooker is now an All-British product, made in England.

The recipes forming the second part of this book have been extracted from AMBROSE HEATH's *Good Food* (Faber and Faber), which may be purchased, price 7s. 6d. net. from all booksellers.

IN PREPARATION BY THE SAME AUTHOR

More Good Food
The Book of the Onion

CONTENTS

11

PART ONE

THE MANAGEMENT AND SCOPE
OF THE AGA COOKER

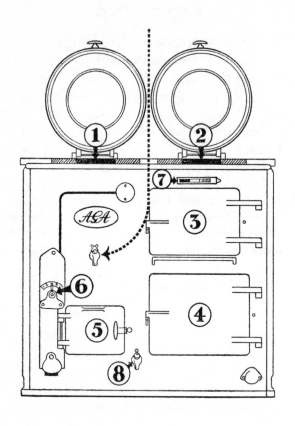

1. THE AGA COOKER

In writing of the AGA Cooker in the pages which immediately follow, it will be necessary to refer to its various parts. The explanatory diagram on the opposite page will be of help here. The different parts will be described separately in later pages.

1. This will be referred to as the left-hand hotplate. It is the hotter of the two cooking surfaces, being used for frying, toasting, grilling and bringing liquids to the boil.

2. The right-hand, or simmering, plate.

3. The fast oven.

4. The slow oven.

5. The ash-pit door.

7. Heat indicator. This must not be regarded as an ordinary thermometer, but only as a gauge for the early morning temperature. The normal reading should be as follows:

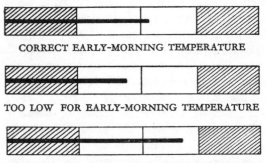

CORRECT EARLY-MORNING TEMPERATURE

TOO LOW FOR EARLY-MORNING TEMPERATURE

TOO HIGH FOR EARLY-MORNING TEMPERATURE

If, first thing in the morning, the mercury is below or above the line in the middle of the white space, the thermostat probably wants adjusting. It does not indicate any danger, but simply means that the fullest efficiency is not being obtained from the cooker. In the ordinary way, the mercury is liable to fall when cooking takes place, but no notice should be taken of this, but only of its position *first thing in the morning*.

If it is *below the line*, you should try turning the thermostat control (6) *one number to the right*. If it is over the line, turn the control *one number to the left*. If this does not result in the mercury being in the right position *the next morning*, you should seek advice from your local agent.

6. The Thermostat Control. The thermostat is an automatic device which reduces the draught when a certain temperature is reached and so prevents the cooker from getting too hot.

8. This is the drain cock of the AGA tank, which contains ten gallons of nearly boiling water. The tap over the ash-pit door gives the supply, but as there is always a certain quantity in the bottom of the tank which is never drawn off, thus ensuring complete safety, a little water should be drained off from this lower tap every few weeks.

The insulating lids to the hot-plates explain themselves. The AGA cooker is a heat storage cooker, and it must be remembered that *open oven doors and hot-plate lids mean that heat is escaping. They should always, therefore, be kept closed as much as possible.*

The ash-pit door must also be kept closed, but for another reason. The draught which feeds the AGA fire is very carefully regulated by the thermostat, but if the ash-pit door is left open, there is an uncontrolled draught which will result in a too rapid consumption of fuel, a far too fierce heat and very likely *damage to the interior of the cooker.*

2. WHAT YOU MUST DO EVERY DAY

One of the greatest advantages of the AGA cooker is the ridiculously small amount of attention that it needs. How little this is will be seen from the following instructions, *which should carefully be adhered to.*

Once the AGA has been lighted, only three operations a day are necessary. It must be 'riddled' night and morning, and filled once a day. (If coke is being used instead of anthracite, it must be filled twice a day.)

Riddling.

The 'riddling' is accomplished thus:

Open ash-pit door.

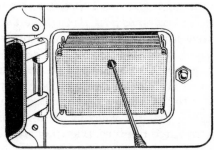

Lift out baffle plate inside.

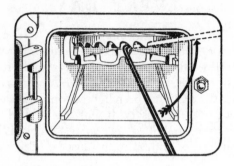

Put the special riddling hook round the spindle of the grate, and lift up so that it fits into the teeth.

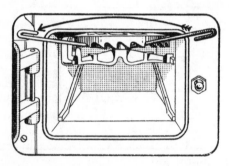

Turn the hook from right to left, and when you have pushed it as far as possible to the left, drop it a little so that it will swing back to the farthest tooth on the right again. Do not rock it backwards and forwards, but keep on turning to the left, till all the loose ashes have dropped through, and it is stiff to turn.

IT IS MOST IMPORTANT TO SEE THAT THE BAFFLE PLATE IS PUT BACK AND THE ASH-PIT DOOR TIGHTLY CLOSED.

Do this once every twelve hours. Nothing could be simpler or cleaner.

EVERY TWENTY-FOUR HOURS, REMOVE THE ASHES AFTER RIDDLING.

Fuelling.

To fill the AGA, you must, *after you have riddled,* lift up the plug in the middle of the left-hand hot-plate, place the special filler over the hole, turn the handle so that the fuel falls through, and continue till no more falls. Take the filler off, *brush off carefully* with the wire brush provided with the stove any dust or pieces on the inside of the ring, and put the cover back again.

This is all you have to do: riddle twice a day, removing ashes once, and fill once a day for anthracite, twice a day for coke.

Cleaning.

The AGA cooker is so finished that it should never really get dirty. If grease and moisture are wiped off with a damp cloth when cooking is in progress, and the ovens are occasionally cleaned with the wire brush, no other cleaning should be needed. The top may, however, be polished now and then with some such polish as Karpol. Do not attempt to clean the bright parts, which only need wiping.

Fuel for the AGA.

The right fuel for the AGA is:

1. Anthracite which will pass through a two-inch ring but not a one-inch ring, or

2. Smallest coke beans. (These should be the size of a small walnut.)

THE AGA COOKER

Cleaning the Flues.

There is one necessary operation which must be performed every three months. This is cleaning the flues; but it is a very different matter from what this term usually implies.

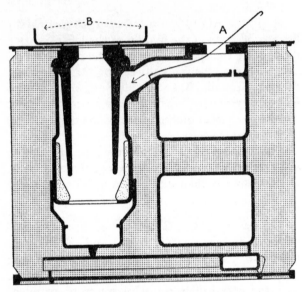

All you have to do (see illustration) is to remove the cover of the right-hand plate and insert in the hole (A) the special soot-rake. Scrape the soot from the back and sides, and push it towards the left so that it falls in the direction of the arrow. Now close up the right-hand plate, and with a special tool (B), which fits into small holes in the top of the left-hand plate, turn the plate to the left as far as it will go, and then to the right, so that it comes back to its original position. Then riddle thoroughly; and that is all.

Removal of Grate.

It is not likely that you will often want to take the grate out altogether, but you might want to remove some clinker or stone. In that case these diagrams will help you.

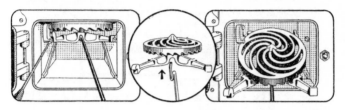

Put the special riddling hook under the grate, with the hook upwards, and at the same time release with a poker the little catch on the left. This can be more easily done if the grate is first pushed forwards.

The grate will then slide out, and you can remove any fuel or ashes that remain.

To replace, slide the grate up on the runners till it engages the catch.

Lighting.

It is even less likely that, with proper attention, the AGA will go out, though it might be necessary to let it go out when holidays are taken. In this event, the grate should first of all be taken out, in the manner described above, so that you can be sure there is no fuel or ash already there. The grate should then be put back, and a crumpled newspaper and a shovelful of *charcoal* put down the barrel through the top of the left-hand hot-plate. Apply a light through the ash-pit door, and leave this open till the charcoal is burning strongly. Then add the usual fuel, replace the baffle plate, and close the ash-pit door.

THE AGA COOKER

It is better not to interfere with the thermostat, but if the cooker is quite cold, it might be turned to one number lower for the first three hours.

———

To keep the AGA at its highest point of efficiency, it is important to remember three things:

ALWAYS KEEP THE ASH-PIT DOOR TIGHTLY CLOSED.

KEEP THE COVERS OF THE HOT-PLATES DOWN AS MUCH AS POSSIBLE.

ALWAYS SEE THAT THE BOTTOMS OF UTENSILS ARE CLEAN AND FREE FROM EXTRANEOUS DIRT AND GRIT.

Once these simple rules have been observed, you will have a perfect and unfailing servant at your command.

3. THE USE AND SCOPE OF THE AGA COOKER IN THE KITCHEN

The secret of the fullest success of the AGA cooker lies in the knowledge of making the utmost use of the various parts of which it is composed. While it is able to perform all the ordinary processes of cooking, it possesses certain features which tend to simplify them, and the use of these must be gained by experience. It is the purpose of the following notes to indicate how these special features can be employed.

THE BOILING PLATE (left-hand hot-plate). The heat on this plate is practically equivalent to a naked flame. On this plate the operations of frying, grilling, toasting and bringing to the boil are performed.

FRYING

Shallow frying, if a quick frying is desired, should be done on this plate. Slower frying is better on the right-hand plate.

Deep frying. It is worth noting that oil or fat will come more quickly to the boil if the pan of oil is first left for some time in the lower oven, and then transferred to the left-hand plate.

GRILLING

A special grilling pan is supplied. This is left on the left-hand hot plate for a few moments until it is really hot. A piece of fat should then be rubbed over the ridges of the grill, and the meat then placed on it and covered with the griller lid, which must remain on during the whole process. A remarkably good grill is thus obtained. (*It is as well to leave the*

THE AGA COOKER

lid of the left-hand hot plate down for at any rate ten minutes before grilling is begun.)

TOASTING

A special toaster is supplied. This is laid on the left-hand plate with the pieces of bread inside it, and should then be covered with the grill cover. If liked, the bread may first be dried a little in the top oven. Very thin toast is best cooked in the top oven, as the plate is a little too fierce. (The lid of the plate may be shut down over the toaster, but the cover of the grill is better.)

BOILING

It will be found that water can be brought very quickly to the boil on the left-hand plate, especially if it is drawn from the AGA tank. A seven-pint kettle of this water will boil in two or three minutes, or cold water in less than ten.

It should be noted that the hottest part of this and the right-hand plates is not the plug, but the solid metal surrounding it. For this reason several saucepans can be kept boiling on the one ring, so long as flat-bottomed pans are used and even a small part of their bottoms is resting on the plate. Adverse comment is sometimes made by the inexperienced on the apparently small cooking surface of the AGA cooker, but it will be shown in later pages that the actual cooking surfaces are much larger than they appear to be.

It is seldom necessary to complete the cooking of boiled food except perhaps green vegetables on the left-hand ring, which is thus left free for frying, etc. There are exceptions to this which will be explained later.

MANAGEMENT AND SCOPE

THE SIMMERING PLATE (right-hand hot-plate). This ring is used for slow cooking and for the transference of utensils after their contents have been brought to the boil on the left-hand plate. Here they will go on simmering indefinitely. The only times when it is inadvisable to use the right-hand plate for this purpose is when a very hot top oven is needed (for this plate robs the oven of some of its heat) or when, as in the case of some green-stuffs and, for instance, rice, a strong boiling temperature is desired. This ring can be used for steaming, and, as has been stated, for slow frying.

THE TOP OVEN. This is used in exactly the same way as any hot oven, but it must be remembered that its temperature varies very little. There is no waning as in an ordinary coal oven, and the heat is more generally applied than in other ovens. The bottom and sides vary little in temperature from the top, a fact which must be borne in mind when cooking on the floor of the oven. There is a very slight increase of temperature at the left-hand side and the back.

THE LOWER OVEN. This oven is the most remarkable feature of the cooker. In action it is very much the same as the old hay-box, and while cooking can be completed in it, foodstuffs can remain covered for a long time without damage. *If the simmering (right-hand) ring is full, or wanted for some other operation, the lower oven can be used instead of it,* thus increasing the 'cooking surfaces'. By the employment of the special flat-lidded pans manufactured for the AGA cooker, a very large amount of food can go into it.

Both these ovens are very deceptive as to size, for owing to their length they are very much larger than they appear to be. For example, a twenty-two pound turkey can be roasted in the top oven.

The principle to be observed with the lower oven is to see that all foodstuffs, the cooking of which is to be completed there, shall be thoroughly heated through before they are transferred either from the left-hand plate or the top oven. The proportionate length of time depends upon the weight and nature of the food, but as the function of the lower oven is to maintain them at their initial temperature, it stands to reason that they must reach this all through before they are put into it. If the lower oven is properly used, it will be found that an enormous amount of labour and attention is saved, for foods such as porridge, hams, stews, stock, soups and sauces can, if covered, either continue to cook or remain there without any attention for many hours at a time, and sometimes overnight.

On no account should the idea be formed that the lower oven is merely a hot cupboard for keeping things warm. If this is done, a great many of the special advantages of the AGA will be missed. Its function is not only to make possible the cooking of many dishes, which are difficult or expensive in other cookers, but also to relieve the hot plates and thus afford a greater use of the top of the stove.

I will return to these special features in the next section, which will deal with the processes of cooking, and will give certain examples of AGA cooking from which a great deal may be learned and important deductions arrived at.

4. UTENSILS

The various uses of the hot-plates and ovens can best be explained by illustration. But first there is an important point to make.

The best results, and the fullest use of the AGA's cooking surfaces, are obtained by always employing *flat-bottomed utensils*. If you look at the bottoms of the various pans you use, you will be surprised to find how 'unflat' they are. And it is important, in order to use, for example, the hot-plates at the maximum efficiency, that the bottom surface should be absolutely flat. The ordinary saucepan usually turns up at the edge.

Special AGA cooking utensils are made with thick heat-conductive bases and a dead flat bottom, and it is strongly urged that for the best results these should be employed. A simple test would be to fill an ordinary saucepan and an AGA saucepan with water, and note the difference of time taken in bringing each to the boil. The same remarks apply to frying-pans and saucepans. Special casseroles in enamelled metal are also supplied.

After careful comparison, I consider it essential that these Special Utensils should be used.

5. THE ORDINARY PROCESSES AND THE AGA COOKER

Only the AGA user will discover for herself the almost unlimited applications of the cooker to the ordinary processes of cookery. A brief outline, and a few suggestions, will put her on the track of full AGA enjoyment.

The times given below are based on the assumption that the AGA is at its average heat, and that, for instance, the insulating lids have not been left open for the whole morning.

BOILING

Vegetables. While all vegetables can be cooked on the top plates, the AGA method is a far better one, as by its use more heat is conserved. This method applies to—Potatoes, Carrots, Turnips, French Beans, Broad Beans, Peas, Asparagus, Parsnips, Seakale, Spinach.

These should first be cooked in the ordinary way on the hot plates (*i.e.* brought to the boil and transferred to the right-hand plate) for ten to fifteen minutes according to the size and age of the vegetable. The water is then strained away completely, the lid put on tightly and the pan transferred to the lower oven for about half an hour. All these vegetables except the potatoes may with advantage have a little butter added to them when they are transferred to the lower oven.

This will be found an ideal way of cooking floury potatoes, as they do not fall to pieces as they are liable to do when boiled.

Green Vegetables. Such as Cabbage, Greens, Leeks Cauliflowers, Brussels Sprouts, etc. must be cooked on the hot plates, as, if they are finished in the oven,

28

they tend to lose colour. They may, of course, be kept hot in the lower oven for a reasonable time.

The first set of vegetables can be left much longer in the bottom oven without being over-cooked, *so long as they are kept covered*. The second set may be kept warm in the same manner for some time.

Dried Vegetables. (Haricot Beans, etc.) These, after having been soaked, should be cooked on the left-hand top-plate for twenty minutes. The water is then drained from them and they should be transferred to the lower oven for forty to sixty minutes.

Puddings. Bring to the boil in the steamer or saucepan on the left-hand hot-plate, and boil hard for ten minutes. Transfer to the simmering plate or lower oven and simmer for the usual time.

Meat and Fruit Suet Puddings on the other hand may be cooked for forty to sixty minutes on the hot-plates, and then, drained of their water but still kept covered, finished in the bottom oven for an hour or an hour and a half according to size.

Christmas Puddings. These should be cooked on the hot-plate for an hour, and then transferred to the lower oven and left there all night, when being made.

Porridge. There is no need to use a double saucepan for this. Cook for ten minutes on the hot-plate, add salt, cover and leave in the lower oven all night.

Stock. Bring the stock to the boil on the left-hand hot-plate, and boil for ten minutes or so. Transfer to the lower oven, well covered, and leave there all night. It will be ready for use in the morning.

Boiled Meat. See under Steaming.

THE AGA COOKER

Fish. Steam in the fish kettle, *in an inch of water*, on the hot-plate for ten minutes or so. Transfer to the lower oven till finished. The time depends upon the size of the fish, but a six-pound salmon would take about three-quarters of an hour in the lower oven.

Fowls. Steam for a quarter of an hour or so on the hot-plate, and transfer to the lower oven for about two hours, according to size and age.

Hams. After the all-important preliminary soaking, hams may be boiled in the usual way, using the lower oven for simmering. They can be excellently steamed in an inch of water in the AGA steamer, allowing one hour on the hot-plate and afterwards twenty-five minutes per lb. in the lower oven. It has been found that hams can be brought to the boil, or steamed for fifteen minutes, and then left in the lower oven all night.

Mutton. Steam or boil for thirty to forty minutes on the hot-plate, and for an hour or two hours in the lower oven, according to size.

Pork. Steam or boil on the hot-plate for forty minutes to an hour, then for one or two hours in the lower oven, according to size.

STEWS AND RAGOUTS

These should be cooked for twenty to thirty minutes on the hot-plate, and then transferred to the lower oven for two or three hours, or even more without harm and often with advantage.

Stewed Fruit should be brought to the boil on the left-hand hot-plate, simmered for a few minutes, and then transferred to the lower oven for twenty minutes or so according to the nature of the fruit.

BRAISING

After the preliminary braising for ten or twenty minutes on the hot-plate, these can be transferred to the lower oven for two or three hours.

FRYING

This can be accomplished, as already explained, in the usual way, either on the left or right-hand hot-plates.

Sautés should be started on the left-hand hot-plate, and then completed in the top oven.

GRILLING

This has already been described on page 23.

ROASTING

If this is done in the top oven only, the times are the same as for any other cooker. In the case of certain meat, such as joints of mutton or beef, it is not necessary to baste, though it is better to do so in the case of chickens and small birds.

If the top oven is wanted for other purposes, the meat may be finished in the lower oven, but it should cook for not less than an hour (over ten pounds, an hour and a half) in the top oven, and then in the lower one for about ten minutes for each pound.

Large joints, and joints of chilled meat, are improved if they are put in the lower oven for half an hour or so before roasting is begun.

The capacity of the top oven may be illustrated by the fact that with the special baking tin supplied, two or three legs of mutton could be cooked at once, or three sirloins or two rolled ribs of about nine pounds each, or six chickens.

If the oven is very full, then a little longer cooking should be allowed, as the number of joints cools the oven rather more at the outset and a little more time has to be allowed for its recovery.

Roast Potatoes can be improved if they are parboiled first or dried in the lower oven for half an hour, then basted with dripping and cooked in the top oven for about an hour.

BAKING

Pies. Fruit pies can be cooked in the top oven for twenty to thirty minutes, according to the nature of the fruit, and then in the lower oven from a half to three-quarters of an hour.

Milk Puddings should be cooked in the top oven for about an hour, and then finished in the lower oven for two hours. They can also be cooked in the lower oven overnight, if they are first cooked for twenty minutes on the left-hand hot-plate or in the top oven. The more slowly they are cooked, the better.

Custards can be baked in the hot oven till they begin to set and brown (about half-an-hour), then moved to the lower oven for about an hour and a half. They can remain there much longer without attention, if necessary, and they can actually be cooked—in about three hours—in the lower oven only. What the French call 'petits pots de crème' are excellently cooked in this way.

Méringues are best baked in the lower oven only for about two hours.

MANAGEMENT AND SCOPE

Baked Potatoes (in their jackets) should be dried in the lower oven for half an hour and then cooked in the top oven for one and a half to two hours.

Soufflés. The top oven is particularly suited to the cooking of soufflés, which should be done in the usual way.

SAUCES

It is in the preparation of sauces that the AGA can be the cook's greatest joy. One of the difficulties of sauces is the inability to keep them hot without a great deal of trouble and the possibility that they may get lumpy and a skin form on them. They are therefore usually made just before the meal is to be served, at the very time when the cook's attention is occupied with other matters.

With the AGA all is different. Sauces can be made and, in most cases, completely finished long before the meal is to be served. They can then be *covered and left in the lower oven*, where they will not only keep free from lumps and skin, but will also improve in flavour. In the case of sauces like oyster or shrimp sauce, the fish must be added at the last minute and not left in the oven with the sauce. I have experimented with this feature of the cooker with great interest, and made sauces several hours before they were needed with complete success.

In the same way, dishes such as fricassées and others in which the meat is introduced into the sauce and cooked there, can be completed in the lower oven in the same successful way.

A Note on the Bain-Marie. It is quite unnecessary, therefore, to employ, for any dishes that usually require it, that cumbersome utensil, the *Bain-Marie*. Vessels which are left in the lower oven *covered* are subjected to exactly the same process as if they were in the *Bain-Marie* itself.

KEEPING DISHES HOT

One of the enormous advantages of the AGA lower oven, is that dishes can be kept hot almost indefinitely without spoiling, so long as they are covered. Even fried food will keep in the lower oven for some time, though it is always best, with all foods, after they have been kept there for some time, to give them a final short heating on a hot-plate or in the top oven.

This removes one of the cook's nightmares—how to keep the second course warm if there is any delay with the service of the first. The unpunctual diner does not suffer as he really deserves to do when an AGA is used, for it makes the service of the courses a very much easier and more reliable matter.

TEMPERATURES

The importance of keeping the insulating lids of the hot-plates closed as much as possible has already been insisted upon. The AGA user will realise the value of this with a little practice, for as the cooker is a heat storage cooker, it must be realised that the careless use of heat will affect the temperature in the ovens, especially the top oven. If a great deal of cooking has been done on the cooker, the temperatures will be slightly lower and allowance will have to be made for this. But *assuming that the usual amount of cooking has been done, and the lids or oven doors have not been left unduly open, the times given above will operate.*

Certain operations are often best done when the cooker has been used, such as those where a lower oven temperature is needed, for example, *cake-making*. It will be found that the best time to make cakes will be after cooking, when the temperature is lower; but if it is desired to lower the temperature of the top oven at any other time, this can be done by leaving the lid of the right-hand hot-plate open for twenty minutes or so and by putting a pan of cold water in the top oven. It is as well to put two or three layers of greaseproof paper over large cakes, and to leave the right-hand hot-plate lid open while they are baking. These precautions are unnecessary with the smaller ones.

Mention has been made of the adverse criticism of cooking space on the AGA cooker. I hope that what I have written will have shown that this is entirely unwarranted, and it will have been seen that a *judicious* use of the hot-plates and the ovens, and especially the lower one, will ensure far greater cooking capacity than on any other stove of its size, or a good deal larger.

If the cooking is planned ahead, as every cook knows it should be, the AGA will not only do all the work required but will very considerably lighten the cook's task. She will find that she will have more leisure, a good deal less work in stoking, cleaning, etc., and it is claimed that her cooking will benefit by AGA advantages. She will have a stove ready for every emergency, a cooker and a small hot water supply at her immediate hand, day or night. The AGA will be always at her service. A dinner party for ten will be almost as simple as breakfast for two, and from being often, in the old fashion, a hot and tedious business, cooking will become a cool and simple pleasure.

6. JAM MAKING AND FRUIT AND VEGETABLE BOTTLING

The following particulars have been supplied by Miss M. S. Frood, M.B.E., Warden of the Helena Club, London.

JAM MAKING

A great deal of trouble in jam making can be saved by the AGA if the preserving-pan containing the fruit and sugar is put into the lower oven till the sugar is melted.

These two jams are specially recommended.

Rhubarb and Marrow Jam. Leave the fruit and sugar in the lower oven all night, then bring rapidly to the boil on the left-hand hot-plate, and boil till the water has disappeared. (Some jam-makers strain this syrup from the fruit and reduce by rapid boiling, then add the fruit and give it a last quick boil.)

Dried Apricot Jam. Five pounds fruit, five pints of water, five pounds sugar, half an ounce bitter almonds. Soak the fruit for some hours, bring to the boil and leave in the lower oven all night. Put on to the left-hand hot-plate and boil till a quarter of the liquid has boiled away, then add the sugar and almonds cut in halves. Boil for about half an hour.

Marmalade. The preliminary cooking of the fruit and water in marmalade is greatly simplified in the AGA, as these can simply be left in the lower oven all night. Here is one of Miss Frood's recipes for Orange Marmalade: Take twelve oranges and cut them into thin circles. Put them into six quarts of cold water and soak till night, then put them into the lower oven and leave till the morning. Put on the left-hand hot-plate, boil till the liquid is reduced

by half, add twelve pounds of sugar and boil fast
for about three-quarters of an hour, or till the marmalade is clear.

FRUIT AND VEGETABLE BOTTLING

The whole process of bottling is much simpler
with an AGA, for as the lower oven remains at an
even temperature, not too hot, bottling can be done
at any time and in any quantity from one to a dozen
3 lb. bottles in one baking. This is all the more convenient, as there may be at hand only a pound or
two of fruit, or not enough for jam or too much for
pies, which can then and there be bottled in the
lower oven without the use of special apparatus.

Any recipe for bottling can be used, provided
that longer times are allowed.

These times, however, will vary slightly according
to the number of bottles placed in the oven at one
time, *e.g.* a whole ovenful will require at least an
hour and a half longer than a single bottle.

METHOD. Before the fruit is placed in the jars, care
should be taken to see that it is handled as gently and
as little as possible. It must be sound and in good
condition, and not too ripe. The jars should be
rinsed out first with hot water, and then with cold.
Pack them, without drying them, with the fruit or
vegetables. Fill to the shoulder with cold water, not
less than an inch and a half from the top, put on the
rubber ring carefully, and place on the lid, clipping
or screwing down. (If it is a screw top, do not screw
it down too tightly.)

When the contents have been cooked, lift the jars
out of the oven, and if using a screw band, screw it
up tightly. Leave them in a cool place and when they

are quite cold unscrew or unclip them. If the process has been successful, the glass lids will be found to be tight and secure, as the sealing is caused by the vacuum created in the jar through the heating and cooling of its contents. If the lids are not tight, then the jars should be re-heated. Before finally placing the screw band on the air-tight lid it should be rubbed with olive oil. The fruit or vegetables thus treated should keep in good condition for a long time, if stood upright in a cool dark place.

When bottled with water, the fruit will require the addition of sugar to taste before use. Some people, however, prefer to bottle the fruit with syrup. In this case, for raspberries and peaches a thin syrup may be made with three-quarters of a pound of sugar (cane sugar is best) to each quart of water. For strawberries, plums and green gooseberries a thicker syrup may be preferred, and then the quantity of sugar should be doubled. The syrup may be made either by pouring boiling water on to the sugar, or by putting the sugar into cold water and boiling it for a minute. In either case it must be allowed to get quite cold before it is added to the fruit.

The following recipes are recommended:

Gooseberries, Strawberries, Raspberries. Top and tail the gooseberries, and take off the stalks of the other fruit. (Small strawberries are better than large ones.) Wash well in cold water. Pack in jars, and proceed as above. Put in the lower oven for four hours.

Cherries. Prepare and wash fruit and pack in jars. Make a syrup (half a pound of sugar to a pint of water) and let it get cold. Fill the jars to the shoulder and cover as above. Put in lower oven for four hours.

Plums. As for Gooseberries, but allow about three hours in the lower oven.

Pears and Apples. These should be peeled and cored, halved or quartered. Allow about five hours in the lower oven.

VEGETABLE BOTTLING

Carrots. Wash well in plenty of water, and blanch in boiling water for a quarter of an hour. Scrape and keep in cold water. Pack into bottles. Cover with cold salted water (proportion: a teaspoonful of salt to a quart of water). Cook in lower oven for nine hours.

Tomatoes. Small are best. Prick in several places before putting in jars. Fill jars to the shoulder with cold water and leave in the lower oven for three hours.

7. BREAD MAKING

Miss Frood has also kindly supplied the following information on Bread Making:

12 lbs. Flour.
12 teaspoonfuls of Salt.
3½ oz. Yeast.
5 pints (about) lukewarm water.
3 teaspoonfuls of sugar.
5 2 lb. tins: 4 2½ lb. tins.

Warm the flour and salt. Mix the yeast and sugar and put it to prove on the top of the cooker with the lids closed. Add yeast and water gradually to the flour and knead very well. Put to rise on the lid of the simmering plate, cover with a cloth, and wait till the dough is twice its original size.

Divide the dough in half, and knead again lightly one half into five equal parts for the smaller tins. Keep the other half warm on the stove. Put the dough in the tins and set to rise again. Knead the other half of the dough for the larger tins whilst the other is rising. The first batch of bread should have risen in about twenty minutes, and can then be put into the oven. Bake for thirty to forty minutes in the top oven, and fifteen to thirty in the lower oven. By the time the first batch is cooked in the top oven, the second batch (which will have been rising) will be ready for baking, and this can now be put in the top oven and left there for an hour to an hour and a quarter. And as the top oven will be slightly cooler by the time the second batch is put in, there will be no need to remove this to the lower oven.

INDEX TO PART ONE

NOTE: *The index to the actual recipes in this book will be found on pages* 235-243.

PART TWO

MONTH BY MONTH RECIPES
FOR THE AGA COOK

taken from Ambrose Heath's *Good Food*

As *Good Food*, the book from which the following recipes were taken, was written for cooks using every sort of cooker, reference should be made to the preceding pages for guidance in regard to special AGA methods, *e.g.* stewing, boiling, etc., when any doubt arises.

FOOD IN SEASON ALL THE YEAR ROUND

FISH

Sea Fish

Bream	Brill
Dory	Flounders
Halibut	Mullet
Plaice	Soles
Turbot	Whiting

Shell Fish

Crayfish	Lobsters
Mussels	Prawns
Shrimps	

MEAT

Beef	Mutton
Veal	

POULTRY

Capons	Chickens
Fowls	Pigeons

VEGETABLES

French Beans	Beetroot
Cabbages	Carrots
Cucumbers	Leeks
Lettuces	Mushrooms
Onions	Potatoes
Tomatoes	Turnips

FRUIT

Apples	Bananas
Grape Fruit	Grapes
Lemons	Oranges
Pineapples	

EMPIRE IMPORTED FRESH FRUIT

Bananas	Pineapples

JANUARY

1. In many of the recipes that follow, *simmering* will be mentioned. Remember that food will simmer just as well in the lower oven as on the simmering (right-hand) hot-plate. To use the lower oven for this purpose not only gives more space on the hot-plate, but, when the hot-plate is not in use, conserves the heat of the stove.

2. It is important to see that the hot-plate lids are always kept down when not in use. Do not keep kettles boiling on the hot-plate. You will only be wasting heat. Remember that the water in the Aga tank is nearly boiling, and will boil up in a minute or two.

3. A wipe in time saves nine. Keep the Aga top clean with a damp cloth as you use it.

> **N.B.**—The flues of the Aga Cooker should be cleaned quarterly (see page 20). Make a note to do so this month.

JANUARY

THE FOOD OF THE MONTH

Food which is in season all the year round is given in the table on page 44.

Note.—Newcomers are printed in italics.

FISH

Sea Fish

Bloaters	Cod
Dabs	Haddock
Ling	Skate
Gurnet	Sprats
Smelts	*Whitebait*

River Fish
Eels

Shell Fish

Oysters	*Scallops*

MEAT
Pork

POULTRY

Ducks	Geese
Turkeys	

GAME

Hares	Leverets
Partridges	Pheasants
Plovers	Ptarmigan
Quails	Rabbits
Snipe	Teal
Doe Venison	Widgeon
Wild Duck	Woodcock

VEGETABLES

Jerusalem Artichokes

Broccoli	Celery
Brussels Sprouts	
Red Cabbages	
Endives	Parsnips
Salsify	Savoys

Seakale
Spanish Onions
Spinach

FRUIT

Cranberries	Medlars
Pears	*Rhubarb*

EMPIRE IMPORTED FRESH FRUIT

Apples	Apricots
Granadillas	Grape Fruit
Lychees	Nectarines
Oranges	Peaches
Pears	Plums

JANUARY

The following recipes are given during this month :

Fish Soup

Whiting
Spinach
Onions
Carrot
Potato
Parsley
Mint
Chives

We do not often eat fish soups in this country, possibly because we have got the idea, from tales of *Bouillabaisse*, that they are too strongly flavoured, or that they are too rich from our experience of the *Bisques* served at our more expensive restaurants.

This simple little soup is perhaps more suited to our northern palates. Chop together a handful of spinach (sorrel instead, if you can get it), one or two small onions, a carrot, a potato, parsley, mint and, if you have them, chives. Brown these in butter and add boiling water, salt and pepper. Into this put a few small whiting whole, and cook for about twenty minutes. Take out the fish, remove their skin and bones; strain the soup and serve with the pieces of fish and vegetables in it.

Garbure

Pickled pork
Haricot beans
Cabbage
Carrots
Bouquet garni

The next soup is a French regional one, and it is rightly famous. There are many ways of preparing it, but here is a fairly easy one. Cook a good handful of well-soaked haricot beans in salted water, and put in a medium-sized cabbage and a few carrots cut in small pieces. Cook on a quick fire and about an hour before you want it, put in a piece of pickled pork, some salt, pepper and a *bouquet* of parsley, thyme and bayleaf. More boiling water can be added to ensure the soup being of the right consistence. The meat and the *bouquet* must, of course, be removed before serving. I am told that peas, or turnips, or potatoes can be substituted for the beans, but the cabbage and pork must be there.

Tomato Soup

Tomatoes
Onions
Water

Tomato Soup is sometimes rather a trouble to make. This version is not.

Cut a couple of large onions in slices and cook them slowly in a little pork fat for a few minutes.

Add half a dozen quartered tomatoes and cook a little longer. Pour on them a pint and a half of boiling water with salt and plenty of pepper. Bring to the boil and simmer till the tomatoes are well cooked. Sieve, and serve, if you care for it, with vermicelli which has been cooked in it for five minutes. Grated cheese might well be added.

The hungry breakfast-eater will welcome a new thrill in the form of Eggs with Ham and Muffins.

Eggs with Ham and Muffins

Split and toast as many muffins as you will need. On each half place a round of fried ham, and on the top a well-drained poached or fried egg. I believe the more adventurous, greatly daring, have been known to add a Sauce Hollandaise, though this seems rather *outré*.

Eggs for luncheon are always nice, Eggs *à la Tripe* especially so. Cook some sliced onions (two for every three eggs) in butter till they are soft, add flour and enough milk to make a thick creamy sauce, and season it with salt, pepper and a little grated nutmeg. Into this sauce put halves, quarters or rings of hard-boiled eggs, and serve piping hot.

Eggs à la Tripe

Eggs
Onions
Milk
Seasoning
Nutmeg

Fresh Haddock can be made very delicious by using a cheese stuffing, which is made by mixing together three ounces of breadcrumbs, two ounces of grated cheese, a tablespoonful of chopped parsley, a good squeeze of lemon juice (or if preferred a dessertspoonful of tomato sauce), salt, pepper and enough beaten egg to bind them. Stuff the fish with this mixture and sew it up. Coat it with the beaten egg left over, sprinkle with browned breadcrumbs, and bake it in the oven with butter or dripping, basting it occasionally. Twenty minutes will do it, and this will give you time to make some Mustard

Stuffed Baked Haddock

Fresh haddock
Breadcrumbs
Cheese
Parsley
Lemon
Egg

Sauce to serve with it. A small cod can be baked in the same way, if the flesh of haddock is thought too dry.

Scallops

Scallops
Tomato
Onion
Mushroom
Parsley
Béchamel sauce

We will cook Scallops by one of the best ways of bringing out their delicious flavour. Boil them in salted water for about fifty minutes, then cut them up small and mix them with a skinned tomato, a very small onion, parsley and one or two mushrooms all chopped together. Cook this for a while in butter, season it well and bind it with a little thick Béchamel sauce. Put it back into the *coquilles*, and brown it in the oven with or without some fresh breadcrumbs sprinkled over. Nor will the grateful gourmand forget that their superior cousin, the delectable oyster (and those from the Delectable Duchy are not to be despised), is but half-way through its season.

Mussel Pilaff

Mussels
Rice
Olive oil
Bacon
Onion
Tomato
Thyme
Bayleaf
Saffron
Parsley
Celery or
Celery salt
White wine
Cheese

Do not be afraid of Mussels in these days of rapid transport, or you will never know the joys of a pilaff of them. It needs a little trouble, but it will be well worth while.

Cook some rice, run cold water over it and let it dry. Now in a little olive oil toss three rashers of streaky bacon which you have first blanched by boiling for a few minutes and then cut in small pieces. Put these aside and cook in the same oil a finely chopped onion, adding two peeled tomatoes cut in slices. When these are soft, season them and add a cupful of hot water, a bayleaf, a little thyme, a pinch of saffron and a lump of sugar.

While this sauce is simmering gently, put a small piece of butter in a saucepan and with it some chopped parsley, a couple of chopped shallots or onions, a small piece of celery (or some celery salt), and half a glassful of white wine. Add the mussels, scraped and cleaned, and cook for six minutes, shaking the saucepan now and then. Strain the liquor and put the mussels back into it. You can leave them in their shells or take them out, as you like. Now take a frying-pan and put all these things into it, the rice, the tomato sauce, the pieces of bacon, the mussels and their liquor, and stir well together till it is very hot, adding a little grated cheese. Serve quickly with more grated cheese sprinkled over it ... and never fear mussels again.

Beef *Strogonoff* has perhaps always seemed an impossibly inaccessible dish for the home, when we have eaten it at our favourite restaurant. In reality it is perfectly easy to make, as the following recipe will show. The only out-of-the-way ingredient is sour cream, which is often at hand by accident when it is least wanted! Cut some slices from a fillet of beef, beat them very flat and cut them into shortish, thin strips. Slice some onions and mushrooms and cook them slowly in butter. When the vegetables are cooked, fry the seasoned slices of beef very quickly in some butter, and add them to the vegetables with thick sour cream. If you want more 'kick' in it, a little French mustard can be included. This dish can be served with the pieces of onion and mushroom left in, but it is perhaps better if the sauce is strained.

Honest and oniony is the following excellent dish. Cook two large sliced onions in butter for a few minutes. Put them with half a pound of sliced potatoes in a buttered fireproof dish with a small teacupful of beef stock, salt and pepper, and cook for about forty minutes in a fair oven. Now brown on both sides some lamb or mutton cutlets, well

Marginal notes:

Beef
Strogonoff

Beef
Onions
Mushrooms
Sour cream
French mustard

Baked Mutton
Cutlets

Cutlets
Onions
Potatoes
Butter
Beef stock

trimmed, and bury them in the potatoes and onions. Finish the dish in the oven, cooking it till the cutlets are nicely done and the potatoes golden brown.

A little experience will tell how long this will take, and how much stock must be added in the first instance to make the dish neither sodden nor too dry, but the literally golden mean between the two.

Goulash of Veal

Veal
Paprika
Onion
Brown stock
Madeira or Sherry
Caraway seeds
Bacon
Potatoes

The Austrians have a pleasant dish called Goulash of Veal, which they cook in this way.

Cut about a pound of veal cutlet into dice, after removing all skin and fat, and season well with salt and pepper and paprika; plenty of the latter. Fry a very small onion finely chopped in a frying-pan in butter, then add the meat and cook slowly for about a quarter of an hour. Now sprinkle on a small spoonful of flour, and pour over a small cupful of brown stock and half a wineglassful of Madeira (or Sherry would do). Add half a teaspoonful of caraway seeds in a muslin bag; or you could leave these out, if you hate the taste of them. Cover it all and leave it to cook gently. Now fry in butter a quarter of a pound of bacon cut into dice, and when it is lightly done add two or three potatoes cut into small cubes, and continue frying till they are golden. Drain them well and add them with the bacon to the contents of the frying-pan. Go on cooking till the meat and potatoes are done, stirring carefully now and then so as not to break the potatoes. Do not forget to remove the little muslin bag before serving this very delicious stew.

Rabbit à la Tartare

Rabbit

Rabbit makes a good January dish. He can most successfully be fried quite plainly in butter and served with more melted butter and chopped parsley, or in a more elaborate fashion, *à la Tartare*, as follows:

Cut him up and let him lie for an hour (half an hour each side) in a marinade of two tablespoonfuls of vinegar, one of olive oil, a small onion cut up, chopped parsley, bayleaf, some mace and a good squeeze of lemon juice. Take him out, dry him, egg-and-breadcrumb him, and fry him in butter. Serve, as the name denotes, with Tartare sauce.

*Vinegar
Olive oil
Onion
Parsley
Bayleaf
Mace
Lemon juice
Egg and
breadcrumbs
Tartare sauce*

Some may prefer a ragout *à l'américaine*. Cut the rabbit up and fry the pieces in butter till they are brown. Drain off the butter, pour in enough stock barely to cover the pieces, put on the lid and cook till tender. Meanwhile make a brown *roux* and mix with it a cupful of tomato purée, fresh or tinned. Take out the rabbit and keep it warm, and add to the *roux* and purée about three-quarters of the stock. Stir them together till they boil, add a pinch of sugar, a large squeeze of lemon juice, salt, and freshly ground black pepper. Put back the rabbit till he is hot again, and serve in the casserole in which he has been cooked.

Rabbit
à l'américaine

*Rabbit
Tomatoes
Lemon juice
Stock*

If we have a little chicken over, and it is not quite enough to make a dish by itself, we should remember Chicken Pancakes.

Toss in butter some small pieces of cold chicken seasoned with salt, pepper and paprika, and, in a separate pan, some mushrooms also cut up small. Bind these together with a very little cream. Make some pancakes with unsweetened batter, stuff them with this mixture, arrange them on a dish, cover them with a Béchamel sauce enriched with the yolk of an egg, sprinkle with grated cheese and brown quickly.

Chicken
Pancakes

*Cooked chicken
Paprika
Mushrooms
Cream
Pancakes
Béchamel sauce
Egg
Grated cheese*

Casserole of
Pigeons

Pigeons
Bacon
Stock
Mushrooms
Claret

A Casserole of Pigeons makes a good luncheon dish in cold weather.

Fry a brace of them in a casserole with a small piece of butter and a rasher of bacon cut into little bits. Add a quarter of a pint of stock, half a pound of small quartered mushrooms tossed in butter, pepper, salt and a good glassful of claret. Cover and simmer very gently till the birds are cooked. When they are ready, strain the sauce, thicken with some brown *roux*, put back the mushrooms and pour over the pigeons.

Partridges en
Cocotte

Partridges
Sausage meat
Bacon
Onion
Carrots

Cook in a casserole for about half an hour some small pieces of bacon and sliced onions and carrots. Take them off the fire and add a tablespoonful of good stock, some salt and pepper. Now put in the partridges, which have been previously stuffed with sausage meat, with a rasher of bacon tied over each. Cook all together with the lid on for an hour or so. When the birds are done, strain the gravy and pour it back over them in the casserole together with some button onions and lean bacon cut in small cubes, which you have meanwhile cooked in butter. Simmer the whole for a little longer, and serve in the casserole.

Brussels
Sprouts with
Chestnuts

Brussels sprouts
Chestnuts
Brown stock
or
Gravy

While Chestnuts are still with us, we must try them with Brussels Sprouts. They make a good, satisfying dish.

Peel and boil some chestnuts. Boil the sprouts for a quarter of an hour, then drain them. Put an ounce of butter, pepper, salt and a little brown stock or gravy into a saucepan, and add the sprouts and chestnuts. Cook for a few minutes together, shaking but not stirring, and serve as hot as possible.

Potatoes are always a problem, but a little inventiveness will soon solve it. Here are three suggestions for enlivening their service.

Melt two and a half ounces of butter in a frying-pan and let it get hot enough to smoke. Then put in four cupfuls of raw potatoes chopped up fairly small. Season them and pack them into as thin a layer as possible. Put a plate over the top and cook slowly till brown and soft.

Brown Hash
of Potatoes

*Potatoes
Butter*

Potatoes *en casserole* are unusual.

Fry in butter, in the casserole you will use, a rasher of bacon cut into tiny cubes. Chop up an onion, fry this a little with the bacon, then add two peeled tomatoes cut in small slices. Now put in some thin slices of cold boiled potatoes, plenty of salt and pepper, a piece of butter and a small teacupful of stock. Mix these ingredients well together, cover, and cook for about twenty minutes in a moderate oven. A tiny piece of garlic finely chopped can be fried with the onion, if the flavour is liked.

Potatoes
en Casserole

*Cold potatoes
Bacon
Onion
Tomatoes
and possibly
Garlic*

Lyonnaise Potatoes are a change from the everlasting *sautées*. *Sautez* some cooked potatoes in butter, and at the same time fry, without browning, some very thin rings of onions in another pan. When the potatoes are nearly done, add the onions to them and brown both together.

Lyonnaise
Potatoes, I

*Cold potatoes
Butter
Onions*

Quite a different way of cooking potatoes *à la Lyonnaise* is as follows. Boil some potatoes in their skins, peel them while hot, slice them and put them into a saucepan. Season them with salt and pepper, and pour over them a purée of onions made by boiling some onions in milk till tender, passing them through a sieve and mixing them with butter and

Lyonnaise
Potatoes, II

*Potatoes
Onions
Milk
Butter*

the liquor they have cooked in till a thin purée results. Heat this up with the potatoes, and serve.

Spinach Soufflé

Spinach
Milk
Butter
Flour
Eggs

A Spinach *Soufflé* makes a pleasant accompaniment to chicken, for instance, and is a delicious course by itself. Cook enough spinach to make two table-spoonfuls of purée. Boil a quarter of a pint of milk with two ounces of butter, and thicken it by adding two ounces of flour and a quarter of a pint of milk which have been mixed smoothly together. Boil this, add the spinach purée with the beaten yolks of two eggs and the whites of four eggs well whipped. It will require thirty minutes cooking in a *soufflé* dish.

Pilaff Rice

Among the recipes in this book Pilaff Rice will occasionally be mentioned. There are various schools of thought on this question, the to-wash or not-to-wash schools, those who introduce the grains into cold water or into boiling water, and so on. They are all agreed, I believe, that the rice to be used should be Carolina and not Patna, which is more suitable as an accompaniment to curries. The principal thing to do is to see, first, that the rice revolves freely and does not catch, and second, that it is put in a sieve under the cold tap immediately it is done, so that the grains are separated. This having been done, you can, of course, add your butter, or your stock, or various flavourings according to the uses for which you intend it. It is sometimes a good tip to boil it with an onion. But you must form your own opinion on this earth-shattering problem: I will not attempt to advise. It is all a matter of tempera-ment, and I am sure that your method is as satis-factory as mine.

But . . . here is a simple pilaff, which will be a stand-by on almost any occasion.

JANUARY

Having boiled the rice according to your lights, and having seen that each grain, more or less, is separate, melt some butter in a frying-pan, put in the rice with a pinch of curry powder, a good pinch of saffron, salt, pepper (black and freshly ground), a pimento cut in small pieces, a few cooked peas, a few soaked and stoned raisins, and then, O then, add whatever 'remains' you wish to sanctify by their inclusion in this noble dish: fish, lobster, prawns, or chicken, or veal, or mutton (not beef, I think). These pieces must have first been just warmed in butter, and then the whole thing is well warmed up and eaten, let us hope with gluttonous ejaculations. If you like, you can add, when you put in your pieces, a small cupful of stock and cook till it has disappeared. Personally, I think this is unnecessary.

A Pilaff of Rice

Rice
Butter
Curry powder
Saffron
Pimento
Peas
Raisins
Stock
'Remains'
of fish or meat

While we are thinking of spicy things, apples with cinnamon have an Eastern atmosphere about them.

Cut some peeled eating apples into quarters, and cook them slowly in a frying-pan in butter, turning them over now and again till they are soft and brown. Sprinkle over them some brown sugar and a little cinnamon, and serve them after they have cooked for just a little longer.

Cinnamon Apples

Apples
Butter
Brown sugar
Cinnamon

We often encounter *Fritto Misto* of Meat in Italian restaurants. A *Fritto Misto* of Fruit seems to be a joyous variation. Simply take pieces of whatever fruits you like: bananas, apples, oranges, pineapples, and so on. Dip them in fritter batter and fry them in deep fat. This might be called Fritters *en surprise*, but you must be careful not to surprise your guests unpleasantly by an injudicious assortment of flavours.

Fritto Misto of Fruit

Crêpes Suzette

Pancake batter
Cream
Oranges
Curaçao
Brandy

Chicken pancakes have, of course, reminded us of another culinary triumph, of which King Edward VII is reputed to have been so fond—*Crêpes Suzette*.

Make a pancake batter to which you have added a liqueur-glassful of curaçao. Set aside for three hours, and just before using add a little cream. Make four pancakes and keep them warm. Now melt in a chafing-dish if possible (for this last operation ought to be done at the table itself) a piece of butter, some sugar and a good squeeze of orange or tangerine juice. When this is melted, put the pancakes in one by one, turn them over once, fold them into four so that they will all lie in the dish, throw over them a liqueur-glassful of brandy and curaçao mixed, set it alight and serve these ambrosial pancakes when the flame dies down.

Angels on
Horseback

Oysters
Bacon

Angels on Horseback might well follow this, for few savouries bear comparison with them. Take some oysters, dust them with a little cayenne pepper, and roll each lovingly in a fragile rasher of streaky bacon. Impale one or two of these delicacies on tiny skewers, and cook them in the oven. The piece of buttered toast which carries these angelic mouthfuls must be the horse.

1. In many of the recipes that follow, *simmering* will be mentioned. Remember that food will simmer just as well in the lower oven as on the simmering (right-hand) hot-plate. To use the lower oven for this purpose not only gives more space on the hot-plate, but, when the hot-plate is not in use, conserves the heat of the stove.

2. It is important to see that the hot-plate lids are always kept down when not in use. Do not keep kettles boiling on the hot-plate. You will only be wasting heat. Remember that the water in the Aga tank is nearly boiling, and will boil up in a minute or two.

3. A wipe in time saves nine. Keep the Aga top clean with a damp cloth as you use it.

> **N.B.—Drain off a pint of water from the bottom tap quarterly. This will prevent sediment accumulating in the bottom of the tank. Make a note to do so this month.**

FEBRUARY

THE FOOD OF THE MONTH

Food which is in season all the year round is given in the table on page 44.

Note.—Newcomers are printed in italics.

FISH

Sea Fish

Bloaters	Cod
Dabs	Haddock
Gurnet	Skate
Ling	Sprats
Smelts	Whitebait

River Fish

Eels   *Salmon*
Trout

Shell Fish

Oysters   Scallops

MEAT

Pork

POULTRY

Ducks	Geese
Guinea-fowl	Turkeys

GAME

Hares	Leverets
Partridges	Pheasants
Plovers	Ptarmigan
Quails	Rabbits
Snipe	Teal
Widgeon	Wild Duck
Woodcock	

VEGETABLES

Jerusalem Artichokes
Broccoli
Brussels Sprouts

Celeriac	Celery
Endive	Parsnips
Salsify	Savoys

Seakale
Spanish Onions
Spinach

FRUIT

Pears   Rhubarb

EMPIRE IMPORTED FRESH FRUIT

Apples	Apricots
Granadillas	Grapes
Grape Fruit	Lychees
Mangoes	Melons
Oranges	Nectarines
Peaches	Pears
Plums	

The following recipes are given during this month:

Mussel Soup

Mussels
Onion
Parsley
Clove
Bayleaf
Thyme
Dry white wine
Cream

Mussel Soup is so cheap that we shall be able to afford the glass of wine we must use in it. Clean the mussels well and cook them for a quarter of an hour or so in a pint of water to which you have added an onion, a good sprig of parsley, a clove, a bayleaf, a little thyme, salt, pepper and a glass of dry white wine. When they are cooked, take them out of their shells and keep them warm. Reduce the soup a little, strain it, and add a little cream, chopped parsley and the mussels.

Peasant Soup

Carrots
Onions
Leeks
Tomatoes
Potatoes
Turnip
Parsley
Peppercorns
A clove
Water
and possibly
Egg
Cream

Here is another simple soup, a slightly more civilised variant of a French peasant soup.

For this you want two carrots, two onions, two leeks, two tomatoes, two potatoes and a small turnip. Slice them all up and fry them for a little in butter. Now add a few sprigs of parsley, a clove, a few pounded peppercorns and, of course, salt, and gradually add enough hot water, which, after boiling for about an hour, will be reduced to the quantity needed. When the soup is cooked, rub the vegetables through a sieve and either serve the soup quite plain or enriched by a tablespoonful of cream, and even still more by the addition of the yolk of an egg added at the last moment. But be sure to use water instead of stock, so as to preserve the simple flavour of the vegetables.

Polish Peasant Soup

Cabbage
Carrot
Turnips
Leeks

Here is another vegetable soup, which needs stock this time. It comes from Poland.

Fry in butter some square-shaped pieces of carrot, turnips, leeks, celery, cabbage, with a pinch of salt and sugar. Add enough brown stock to satisfy the expectant appetites, and simmer for an hour or so. Remove grease, and thicken with some browned

FEBRUARY

flour mixed with a little stock. Boil up again, and after the soup has been taken off the fire, stir in a little cream.

Celery
or
Celery salt
Brown stock
Cream

Devilled Eggs can be prepared in two ways at any rate. Here they are.

Cook the eggs in butter in an omelette pan, turning them over once, but seeing that they are not cooked too much (the yolks should be soft) and do not break. Slip them on to the serving dish, and pour over them some brown butter with a few drops of vinegar.

Devilled
Eggs, I

Eggs
Brown butter
Vinegar

The second way is to hard-boil some eggs, cut them in half lengthwise, and fill them with their own yolks mixed with butter, plenty of cayenne pepper and salt. Serve them very hot with a sauce made of thick brown gravy mixed with two tablespoonfuls of Worcester sauce and a dessertspoonful of French mustard. A little chopped parsley is a pleasant adornment.

Devilled
Eggs, II

Hard-boiled
eggs
Butter
Cayenne
Brown gravy
Worcester
sauce
French
mustard
Parsley

Birds' Nests are amusing for breakfast, especially if there are children about. Cut some slices of bread an inch thick and cut it out in rounds. Stamp out the centres with a smaller cutter so as to make rings. Fry these in butter till golden. Put them into a fireproof dish, break an egg into each, pour over a few drops of cream or milk, sprinkle with salt and pepper, with a little chopped parsley and (if you can face it early in the morning) some chopped onion, and bake in the oven till the eggs are set.

Birds' Nests

Eggs
Bread
Butter
Cream or Milk
Parsley
and possibly
Onion

In Brittany they have a pleasant way of cooking Cod in Cider.

Skin and bone the cod, and cut it into pieces. Put them into a casserole with a tablespoonful of

Cod in Cider

Cod
Olive oil
Cider

Butter
Flour
Parsley
Shallot
Mushrooms

olive oil and a pint of dry cider. Season with pepper and salt. Add a piece of butter about half the size of an egg which you have mixed with a little flour and parsley, shallot (or onion) and mushrooms finely chopped together. Cook all this quickly over the flame, so that the fish is done and the sauce suitably reduced at the same time.

Sole Otéro

Baked potatoes
Butter
Sole
Shrimps
Sauce Mornay

Baked Potatoes (in the jackets) are always popular, but decidedly so when they form part of Sole Otéro.

Bake as many large potatoes as you want, cut a hole in the side of each and scoop out the contents, so as to leave the skins unbroken. Mash the potato with butter, salt and pepper. Meanwhile you have cooked some fillets of sole in the oven. These you now cut up into small pieces, mix them with some picked shrimps and moisten with Sauce Mornay. Mix this with the potato purée, refill the skins with the mixture, and heat them up again in the oven.

Brochet of
Oysters

Oysters
Butter
Cream
White wine
Anchovy
essence
Lemon rind
Parmesan
Breadcrumbs

A light dish of Oysters can be provided as follows. Heat two ounces of butter and a quarter of a gill of cream in a stewpan, and stir in a small wine-glassful of Chablis, a tablespoonful of anchovy essence and some grated lemon rind. Pour half of this mixture into a fireproof dish and lay some large oysters, minus their beards, upon it. Sprinkle with grated Parmesan cheese and breadcrumbs, pour over the remainder of the sauce, add salt and pepper, more breadcrumbs and cheese, and bake briskly till browned. Serve very hot in the same dish.

Scallops
au gratin

Scallops
Béchamel sauce

Scallops *au gratin* are a simple and digestible dish for invalids and others. Wash the scallops well and cook them gently for at least half an hour in a good white sauce. Pour it all into a buttered fireproof dish, sprinkle with breadcrumbs, or breadcrumbs and grated cheese, pour over a little melted butter and brown in the oven.

Breadcrumbs
Grated cheese
Butter

A real *Wiener Fleischschnitt* is a very different matter from the lugubrious mixture of bread and meat and gravy with lank and greasy fried onions which we know as Vienna Steak in this country. Chop very finely about two pounds of lean beef, and mix it well with a teaspoonful of chopped parsley, the same of powdered mixed herbs, a grating of nutmeg, salt, pepper, the yolk of one egg and one whole egg beaten together. Shape into flat oblong cakes, flour them and fry them in a little butter till they are cooked; then drain them and keep them warm. Meanwhile cut a large onion into rings. Coat these with flour, dip them in the beaten white of egg that you have left, again in the flour, and fry them in deep fat till lightly browned. Serve the steaks garnished with the rings and with a brown sauce. This is the best way of cooking fried onions, say for steak and onions.

Vienna Steak

Beef
Parsley
Mixed herbs
Nutmeg
Eggs
Butter
Onion
Flour
Brown sauce

Fried Onions

For cold days and hungry mouths Brain and Tongue Pudding is the very thing.

Soak four sheeps' brains and four sheeps' tongues in salt and water for two or three hours, then simmer the tongues in stock or water until the skins can be taken off. Line a basin with suet paste and put in alternate layers of sliced tongue and coarsely chopped brains, seasoning each layer with finely chopped shallot, or onion, and parsley, salt and pepper. Put in here and there some slices of hard-boiled egg. Pour in a quarter of a pint of milk, cover with suet, tie up and steam for three and a half hours.

Brain and
Tongue
Pudding

Sheeps' brains
Sheeps' tongues
Stock or Water
Suet paste
Shallot or Onion
Parsley
Hard-boiled egg
Milk

Veal à la Crème

Veal is very good now, and there are a hundred ways of serving it. One of the simplest and most exquisite is *à la crème*, for which you take some thin slices of fillet, well beaten, and cook them in a frying-pan in butter. When they are nicely brown, take them out and keep them hot. Scrape the pan well so as to mix the butter and the juices which have escaped from the meat, season well, and add some fresh cream. Cook a little longer and pour this over the slices. This is the best way of capturing the individual but somewhat elusive flavour of veal. Only a little potato with this, purée for choice, but a squeeze of lemon may be permitted.

Creole Ragout of Veal

Veal
Ham
Potatoes
Onions
Carrots
Lard
Garlic
Flour
Tomatoes
Vinegar
Parsley
Thyme
Bayleaf
Marjoram
Cayenne
Water

This is a very savoury Creole fashion of cooking veal.

Cut three pounds of brisket of veal into two-inch squares, half a pound of lean ham and four medium potatoes into cubes, and two large onions and two medium carrots into slices. Melt a tablespoonful of lard in a saucepan and fry the veal, seasoned with salt and pepper, till it is brown. Then add the other ingredients already prepared, with a minced clove of garlic, and let them brown together. Now mix in a tablespoonful of flour, six fresh tomatoes cut in slices, a teaspoonful of vinegar, some chopped parsley, thyme, bayleaf and marjoram, a little cayenne pepper, and a quart of water. Cover closely and let it simmer for about two hours, when it will be ready for your delectation.

Sausages with Cabbage

Boiled pickled-pork liquor
Cabbage

One of the famous ways of cooking sausages is with cabbage.

For this you need the liquor in which you have boiled some pickled pork with a *bouquet* of parsley, thyme and bayleaf. Bring it to the boil and throw

FEBRUARY

in your cabbage cut in fairly small pieces. When the cabbage is half cooked, you should have ready some grilled sausages, the kind called Parisian sausages being the best. Drain the cabbage and chop it up with some more pepper, a little grated nutmeg and a small piece of butter. Lay half the cabbage in a fireproof dish, put in the sausages and cover them with the rest of the cabbage. Pour over a cupful of beef stock, put on the lid and cook for another half-hour in a moderate oven.

Sausages
Nutmeg
Butter
Beef stock
Bouquet garni

Another famous dish, this time Spanish, is *Arroz à la Valencia*, a mixture of fish and meat which sounds strange to us but 'eats well', as they say.

Cook in white stock some chicken, pieces of ham, some tiny sausages and pieces of fish, all cut in small cubes. While these are cooking, chop together a large onion, some parsley and a small piece of garlic, and brown them in a deep pan in a couple of table-spoonfuls of olive oil. Add as much Patna rice as you will need and brown it lightly. Then put in two pimentoes previously fried and two peeled tomatoes, all cut into small pieces. Cook a little more, stirring now and then with a wooden spoon, and season with salt, black pepper and a little pounded cloves. Now put in the pieces of fish and meat and the little sausages cut in rounds. Add the stock they have been cooked in by degrees, but do not stir any more, only shaking the pan now and again. It is finished when the rice is cooked and the stock absorbed. Cooked mussels in their shells can be used to garnish this extraordinary mixture, or pieces of lobster, or prawns, or the chicken may be in larger pieces.

Arroz à la
Valencia
(Spanish
Rice)

White stock
Chicken
Ham
Sausages
Fish
Onion
Parsley
Garlic
Olive oil
Patna rice
Pimentoes
Tomatoes
Cloves
Mussels
or possibly
Lobster
Prawns

Chicken can be stewed with chestnuts to advantage. Divide a fowl into the usual pieces and brown

Stewed
Chicken with
Chestnuts

67

Chicken
Water
Chestnuts

them in about an ounce of dripping. Pour in enough water for them to stew in, and simmer for three-quarters of an hour. Then add salt and pepper and a dozen or so chestnuts previously peeled and skinned. Cook slowly for another hour, or longer if the ingredients are not quite done. Dish up, reduce the sauce and pour it over the chicken and chestnuts.

Gibelotte of
Rabbit

Rabbit
Pork or Bacon
fat
Shallots
or Onions
Parsley
White wine

Before Rabbit goes out of season, let us eat him in a *Gibelotte*.

Joint him and fry the pieces, till they are about half cooked, in pork or bacon fat. Fry also a few chopped shallots or onions in the same fat and mix them with the pieces of rabbit, some chopped parsley, salt and pepper, and a glass of white wine, preferably Sauterne. Simmer this all for half an hour or so, when it will be ready.

Gibelotte of
Mutton

Mutton
Pork or Bacon
fat
Shallots
or Onions
Parsley
White wine

This is also a good way of using up roast lamb or mutton, by simply browning the slices and substituting them for the pieces of rabbit: another revelation in the method of avoiding the ubiquitous hash.

Salmi of
Wild Duck

Wild duck
Claret
Port
Stock
Butter
Flour
Brandy
Lemon juice
Cream

This kind of Salmi makes Wild Duck rather more interesting.

Roast the duck, basting it well, in a quick oven for about twenty minutes. It must not be quite done. Keep it warm and make a sauce with a tablespoonful of claret and the same of port, a very little stock, a walnut of butter mixed with flour, reduced to half. Fillet the duck and *flambez* the fillets with brandy. Keep them warm while you add to the sauce any blood and gravy from the dish in which the duck was roasted and carved, a squeeze of lemon juice and a little fresh cream. Reduce slightly again, and strain carefully over the fillets.

FEBRUARY

Fried Jerusalem Artichokes offer a change from the usual garnishings for grills. Either cut them, raw, into thin slices and fry them quickly in deep fat, sprinkling the pieces with salt and pepper before serving; or fritter them in a batter made with two tablespoonfuls of flour, the same of milk, one table-spoonful of salad oil and the yolk of an egg, which has been allowed to stand for some time after being made.

Fried Jerusalem Artichokes

This is an Italian way of cooking Leeks.

Trim and divide the leeks into pieces about two inches long, and soak them in cold water for an hour. Then cook them in boiling salted water till they are tender, take them out and leave them again in cold water for another hour at least. Drain them and dry them at the end of this time and cook them again gently in two ounces of butter for ten minutes. Have some hot Béchamel sauce ready, and add to it a dessertspoonful of grated Parmesan cheese, salt, pepper, and the yolk of an egg. Mix this well together, arrange the leeks in a fireproof dish, pour the sauce over them and bake in a moderate oven till brown.

Italian Leeks

Leeks
Butter
Béchamel sauce
Parmesan
Egg

Now for three ways of cooking potatoes.

Cut the potatoes into small pieces about an inch square, and fry them slowly in butter, or bacon fat, till they are well done and all the fat is absorbed. Just before finishing, sprinkle with some chopped parsley and, possibly, garlic.

Peasant Potatoes

Potatoes
Butter or Bacon fat
Parsley
and possibly Garlic

An unusual potato purée, which is particularly good with any meat or fish dishes which require an orange accompaniment, can be made by adding the juice and grated rind of an orange to an ordinary

Potato and Orange Purée

69

purée. Mix it well together and serve with a little more grated rind on the top. It is pretty, and surprisingly good.

Potatoes à la
Dauphinoise

*Potatoes
Egg
Nutmeg
Milk
Gruyère cheese
and possibly
Garlic*

This is a pleasant potato dish. Put two pounds of thinly sliced raw potatoes into a basin with a beaten egg, salt, pepper, grated nutmeg, a pint and a half of boiled milk and a quarter of a pound of grated Gruyère cheese. Mix together well, pour into a well-buttered dish (which you have perhaps rubbed round with garlic), sprinkle with a little more cheese, and bake in a moderate oven for about three-quarters of an hour.

Banana
Soufflé, I

*Bananas
Flour
Sugar
Milk
Eggs
and possibly
Icing sugar*

Here are two recipes for Banana *Soufflé*.

One. Cut four large bananas in half lengthwise, keeping the skins intact. Mash the flesh through a fine sieve. Now mix a level tablespoonful of flour and the same of castor sugar in a breakfast-cupful of hot milk. Bring it to the boil and cook a little longer, stirring well. When it is thick, add the yolks of two eggs, a small piece of butter, the stiffly whipped whites of three eggs, and the mashed bananas. Fill the banana skins with this mixture, and bake for about eight minutes in a hot oven. A little icing sugar can be sprinkled over each just before they are ready.

Banana
Soufflé, II

*Bananas
Milk
Sugar
Eggs
Oranges*

Two. Boil half a pint of milk with eight lumps of sugar. When it is cold, stir in the beaten yolks of two eggs. Mash well together the flesh of six bananas and of two sweet oranges (all pips and pith must be removed from the latter). Add this mixture to the milk and eggs, and fold in the whites of the eggs stiffly beaten. Pour into a buttered *soufflé* dish and bake in the oven in a tin of water till browned.

FEBRUARY

This unusual kind of fritter I first tasted in a little
Smyrnese restaurant in London. The proprietor
called them *Loucoumathes*, which I am told is a
Turkish term of endearment. They certainly de-
served it.

Warm half a pound of flour and a quarter of a
pint of milk. Put the flour into a bowl and make a
hole in the middle of it. Now mix a quarter of an
ounce of yeast with half a teaspoonful of sugar, add
the milk to this and pour it into the centre of the
flour. Mix, and when it has 'sponged', beat in three
yolks of egg and leave it for three-quarters of an
hour. Knead the mixture well and let it rest for
another ten minutes. It is then ready to be dropped,
in tablespoonfuls, into smoking hot fat and eaten
as quickly as possible with warm honey and powdered cinnamon.

Loucoumathes

Flour
Milk
Yeast
Sugar
Eggs
Honey
Cinnamon

Let us think of something light for a change.
This orange salad will do excellently.

Cut some oranges into slices, removing the pips
and pith, but carefully preserving the escaping juice.
Put the slices into a glass dish, and pour over them a
thin syrup which you have made from the juice (with
more added, if needs be) and castor sugar. Melt a
quarter of a pound of lump sugar with half a tumbler
of water in an enamelled pan, and boil it for about
ten minutes till it is a lightish caramel. Pour it out on
a dish to cool and, when it is cold and stiff, crush it
rather coarsely. Sprinkle it over the fruit, cover with
whipped cream, which in its turn should be adorned
with splintered burnt almonds. The addition of a
little liqueur, to your taste, to the oranges would
be an undoubted improvement.

Orange Salad

Oranges
Sugar
Cream
Burnt almonds
and possibly
Liqueur

71

Cheese
Pancakes, I

Batter
Cheese

Cheese Pancakes are the antithesis to the *Crêpes Suzette* of last month, but they are seldom encountered in England even on Shrove Tuesday. Two varieties have come to my notice.

The first is made simply by the addition of some grated cheese with the uncooked unsweetened batter. After you have made the pancakes in the ordinary way with this mixture, just sprinkle a little more cheese over them.

Cheese
Pancakes, II

Batter
Gruyère cheese
Sugar
Eggs

The second is richer. Have ready four pancakes made with unsweetened batter. On the first spread a layer of a mixture of grated Gruyère cheese, a little salt, a little sugar and the yolks of four eggs stirred smoothly together. Then another pancake, more mixture, and so on, the last pancake being on top. This heap you cut into quarters and cook them in butter. Some add more melted butter, but as the Elephant's Child said, that would be 'too buch for be'.

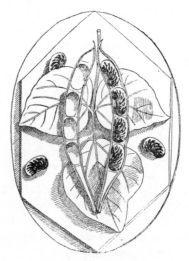

IMPORTANT POINTS TO REMEMBER

1. In many of the recipes that follow, *simmering* will be mentioned. Remember that food will simmer just as well in the lower oven as on the simmering (right-hand) hot-plate. To use the lower oven for this purpose not only gives more space on the hot-plate, but, when the hot-plate is not in use, conserves the heat of the stove.

2. It is important to see that the hot-plate lids are always kept down when not in use. Do not keep kettles boiling on the hot-plate. You will only be wasting heat. Remember that the water in the Aga tank is nearly boiling, and will boil up in a minute or two.

3. A wipe in time saves nine. Keep the Aga top clean with a damp cloth as you use it.

73

MARCH

THE FOOD OF THE MONTH

Food which is in season all the year round is given in the table on page 44.

Note.—Newcomers are printed in italics.

FISH

Sea Fish

Bloaters	Cod
Dab	Gurnet
Ling	Skate
Smelts	Sprats
Whitebait	

River Fish

Eels	Salmon
Trout	

Shell Fish

Oysters	Scallops

MEAT

Lamb	Pork

POULTRY

Ducklings	Ducks
Guinea-fowls	
Turkeys	

GAME

Hares	*Ortolans*
Ptarmigan	Rabbits
Wild Duck	Woodcock

VEGETABLES

Jerusalem Artichokes
Broccoli
Brussels Sprouts

Celeriac	Endive
Parsnips	*Radishes*
Salsify	Savoys

Seakale
Spanish Onions
Spinach
Spring Onions
Watercress

FRUIT

Pears	Rhubarb

EMPIRE IMPORTED FRESH FRUIT

Apples	Granadillas
Grapes	Grape Fruit
Mangoes	Melons
Nectarines	Oranges
Peaches	Pears
Plums	Pomegranates

74

The following recipes are given during this month :

Watercress
Soup

*Watercress
Potatoes
(If liked
Cream,
Egg and
Lemon juice)*

This is a recipe for Watercress Soup.

Cook a pound of floury potatoes till they are about three-quarters done, then add a bunch of watercress well washed and chopped. When the potatoes are done, strain them and the cress through a wire sieve and put this purée back into the saucepan with some water and cook a little longer without boiling. Cream can be added, and the yolk of an egg beaten with lemon juice. You can adorn it with a few chopped leaves of the cress and, as it is a thick-thin soup, with tiny squares of fried toast.

Soupe Maigre

*Lettuce
Spinach
Parsley
Butter
Egg*

For the more spring-like days, a lighter soup may be preferred. For instance, a *soupe maigre*; useful for Lent, too.

Cut two lettuces and a handful of spinach into strips and cook them with a chopped handful of parsley in some butter till they are very soft. Add hot water, salt and pepper, bring to the boil and simmer for about three-quarters of an hour. Beat the yolk of an egg (or of two) and stir into the soup when it comes to the table.

Eggs in Rolls

*Eggs
Breakfast rolls
Anchovy
essence*

Here are two ways of cooking Eggs, the first for hearty breakfast-eaters.

For this you need morning rolls from which you have scooped out the indigestible inside. Butter them well inside and spread them with a mixture of chopped hard-boiled egg, anchovy essence and pepper, in the proportion of one egg and a dessert-spoonful of essence to each roll. Put the halves together again and bake till very hot.

Stuffed Eggs
(hot)

Cut some hard-boiled eggs in half lengthwise. Take out the yolk and mix it with some mushrooms

MARCH

(first fried lightly in butter) and tongue or ham chopped together; bind with a little cream. Stuff the eggs with this, arrange them on a bed of spinach, sprinkle with cream and some grated cheese, pour over a little melted butter and brown quickly.

Hard-boiled eggs
Mushrooms
Tongue (or Ham)
Cream
Spinach
Cheese

Now for the Fish. First, four ways of making Salt Cod more exciting. It is assumed that the cod has first been sufficiently soaked.

The first is simply to cut the cod into squares, roll them up and bind them with string, and boil in the usual way. Remove the string, and dish them up sprinkled with roughly chopped parsley and lemon juice and covered with lightly browned butter, or black butter, if you prefer it. Boiled potatoes with this, please.

Salt Cod
au beurre
noisette

Salt Cod
Parsley
Lemon juice
Butter

The second is to boil a pound of the fish, and when it is cooked flake it and mix with about three-quarters of a pint of Sauce Indienne. Rice can be served with this. Sauce Indienne is made with butter and flour, a little saffron, a pinch of curry powder, milk, salt, pepper and grated nutmeg, and should have the consistency of cream.

Salt Cod
à l'indienne

Salt cod
Sauce Indienne

The third is a Creole variation. Fry a minced onion in butter till golden, spread it on the bottom of an earthenware dish, and on it place three or four tomatoes which have been first fried and then finished in the oven sprinkled with chopped parsley, breadcrumbs and a suspicion of garlic, that is, *à la provençale*. Now take your flaked boiled cod, place it on the tomatoes, surmount the whole with three or four pimentoes (tinned ones will do very well), anoint with slightly browned butter and a squeeze of lemon, and heat well in the oven.

Salt Cod
à la créole

Salt cod
Onion
Tomatoes
Parsley
Garlic
Breadcrumbs
Pimentoes
Butter
Lemon

77

Salt Cod aux
Œufs

Eggs
Butter
Lemon

The fourth, Salt Cod cooked with eggs, is really admirable. You make it by first boiling your cod (after it has been well soaked, of course) till it is cooked. Break the flesh into small pieces and keep it hot. Now melt a good piece of butter in a frying-pan, put into it six eggs beaten together and cook slowly, stirring well as you would for *œufs brouillés*. While it is solidifying, put in the pieces of fish, some more butter, pepper, and the juice of half a lemon. Do not keep this dish waiting: any delay in eating is fatal to its charm.

Tripe Wiggle

Tripe
Flour
Butter
Milk
Oysters

Before Oysters go out of season, there is an unusual way of serving them which deserves to be tried.

Cut a pound of cooked tripe into small pieces and add them with a good number of oysters to a white sauce made of flour, butter and half a pint of milk and tripe liquor mixed. Season this carefully and cook together for a little while. It is a noble combination.

Salmon à la
Bretonne

Salmon
Butter
Mushrooms
Parsley
Lemon juice

Salmon has been with us long enough for a slight change in his manner of presentation to be made.

Cut the flesh into cubes of about one-inch sides, season them, and *sautez* them in butter with a few small fresh mushrooms. Half cook these pieces on the flame, then put the pan in the oven and let them finish cooking there. Drain them, and serve sprinkled with parsley and with a sauce of lightly browned butter and a little lemon juice.

Braised
Duckling
with
Turnips

This is the classical way of preparing *Caneton braisé aux Navets*.

Brown the duckling in butter and take it from the

saucepan. Drain away the butter and pour in two-thirds of a pint of brown stock, the same of Espagnole sauce, a drop of white wine, and a *bouquet* of parsley, thyme and bayleaf. Put the duck back in this and braise gently for about two hours.

In the butter in which the duckling has been browned cook a pound of baby turnips of the size of a cherry-plum (or, if they are larger, cut them to the size of a very large olive) and sprinkle them with a good pinch of powdered sugar so that they are a nice golden brown when finished. Cook also in butter twenty or so button onions.

When the duckling is half cooked (that is, after about an hour), take it out, put it into another saucepan with the turnips and onions, strain the sauce over it, and complete the cooking.

Serve garnished with these vegetables.

Duckling
Brown stock
Espagnole sauce
White wine
Parsley
Thyme
Bayleaf
Turnips
Button onions

Here is a recipe for *Petit Poussin à la Polonaise*. To cook these tender youngsters in this fashion exalts them to a high place in the gastronomic hierarchy.

Stuff each of the birds with a forcemeat made of veal, bacon, liver, a little onion, parsley, a hint of thyme and the ghost of bayleaf incorporated with breadcrumbs soaked in a little stock and some butter. Fry them briskly in butter to brown them slightly and finish cooking them in a *cocotte*.

For serving, cut them in half and keep them hot, having sprinkled them with the hot yolks of two hard-boiled eggs chopped up with some parsley. Meanwhile melt in a frying-pan a couple of ounces of butter. When this is foaming, throw in a table-spoonful of fresh breadcrumbs, fry for a second or two and pour over the *poussins*.

Poussin à la
Polonaise

Baby chicken
Forcemeat of
veal
Bacon
Liver
Onion
Parsley
Thyme
Bayleaf
Butter
Eggs
Breadcrumbs
Stock

Woodcock à la fine champagne

Woodcock
Brandy
Game fumet
Lemon juice

The Woodcock *à la fine champagne* is an almost inexcusable luxury, but that should not discourage us once in a while.

Having roasted the undrawn woodcock (a little underdone), cut it into six pieces—the wings, the legs and the two halves of the breast—which you will keep hot.

Now finely chop up the intestines and press the carcase on to a pan so as to squeeze out any blood. Remove the carcase and *flambez* the rest with a glass of brandy. Reduce a little, add a tablespoonful of game *fumet*, or stock, a squeeze of lemon juice and a little cayenne pepper. Pour this mixture over the pieces of the bird and serve them surmounted by the woodcock's head.

Woodcock à la Riche

(As above with foie gras)

You can serve the pieces, if you like, on toast on which the cock has been roasted, or enrich the dish still further by thickening the sauce with a little purée of *foie gras* and an ounce of butter (*à la Riche*).

Chicken au Gratin

Cooked chicken
Mashed potato
Béchamel sauce
Cheese

If we have any cold chicken over, do not let us forget one of the simplest ways of adorning it.

Cut the chicken into small pieces. Put them in a buttered fireproof dish in which you have first built a wall of mashed potato. Cover them with Béchamel sauce, sprinkle with grated cheese and brown in the oven.

Beef Gratiné

Cold Beef
Onions
Tomatoes
Parsley
Breadcrumbs
Stock

For disposing of cold beef, try this way.

Chop up some onions—fairly finely—fry them in butter, but do not let them brown. Add the beef cut in thinnish slices, and cook again for a few minutes. Arrange the meat on the chopped onion in the dish in which you will serve it, pour over a tablespoonful of stock, a little tomato sauce (or purée will do, if you are in a hurry). Add chopped parsley, salt and pepper. Now sprinkle fairly liberally with breadcrumbs, dot with butter, and brown well in the oven. You can wall this in with potato, too, if you like.

Mutton can be treated advantageously in the same way.

Mutton Gratiné

Grilled pork chops *à la Maréchale* must not be missed before pork 'goes out'.

Grill the chops, and just before bringing them to the table, make a few small gashes on one side and spread a mixture of butter, chopped parsley, pepper and salt. Serve an orange sauce separately.

Pork Chops à la Maréchale

Pork chops
Butter
Parsley
Orange sauce

Orange sauce also plays a part in Veal Cutlets *à la Maréchale*.

Brush the veal cutlets with the yolk of an egg and roll them in a mixture of half fine breadcrumbs, half Parmesan cheese. Fry them a golden brown and serve with a purée of spinach, and with an orange sauce poured over the cutlets.

Veal Cutlets à la Maréchale

Veal
Egg
Breadcrumbs
Parmesan cheese
Butter
Spinach
Orange sauce

Braised veal is more interesting than roast.

Your piece of veal, weighing about three pounds, should first be browned on all sides in butter. To this butter, when the veal has been temporarily removed, add half a dozen carrots cut in slices, the same number of button onions, a little parsley, a rasher of bacon—not too thin—cut in small bits and, of course, salt and pepper. Put in a tablespoonful of water and the veal, and cook in the oven with the lid on, shaking the dish now and then. Serve with potato croquettes, in the mixture of which you have added a little cheese.

Braised Veal with Carrots

Veal
Carrots
Onions
Bacon
Parsley

Potatoes are sometimes a problem when we are all wishing it was time for new ones. The following is an excellent and simple way of cooking them.

Potatoes Anna

Potatoes
Butter

See that the potatoes are cut into evenly thin rounds—raw, of course. Let them lie in water for ten minutes or so; then dry them, and as they are dried arrange them in layers in the buttered dish in which they are to be cooked. Between each layer of potato put some little pieces of butter (do not begrudge this), and pack the layers tightly. Fill the dish to the top, over which spread some more butter. Now make the lid of the dish airtight with a paste of flour and water, and bake in a slow oven for fifty minutes. Take out the dish and, after cutting the cake in four and turning it upside down, put on the lid and cook again for another ten minutes. Serve with the melted butter poured over.

Hungarian Potatoes

Potatoes
Onion
Tomatoes
Butter
Paprika
Stock
Parsley

The Hungarian method of cooking potatoes is a good one too.

Fry four ounces of chopped onion in butter, adding a coffeespoonful of paprika. Add two peeled tomatoes, sliced, and two pounds of rather thickly sliced potatoes. Just cover with stock and cook in the oven till the stock has practically disappeared. At the last minute sprinkle with chopped parsley.

Poires Flambées

Pears
Sugar
Vanilla pod
Liqueurs

March is not a good month for fruit, but South Africa sends us pears and peaches which, if they are not really first-class dessert fruit, are very good to 'flamber'. Thus they make an imposing-looking dish, which is really very easy to produce for the excitement and appreciation of your less-sophisticated friends.

See that the pears are unbruised, peel them, and prick them all over with a needle. Stand them in just enough water to cover them, to which you have added some sugar and a vanilla pod. Bring to the boil and cook about half an hour in a moderate oven. They should be quite soft and white, but whole. Serve them on a hot metal or glass dish, and when they come to the table pour over them a small glassful of liqueur which has been slightly warmed and set it alight. Maraschino and brandy (half and half) is perhaps the best mixture, but experiments can advantageously be made with others.

An Apple Tart cooked in the German fashion is a pleasant change for luncheon.

Apple Tart

Apples
Pastry
Lemon
Mixed spice
Egg
Milk
Almonds

To an ounce of melted butter add the juice of half a lemon, two tablespoonfuls of castor sugar, half a teaspoonful of mixed spice and an egg beaten up with a cupful of milk. Mix this well together and put in a pound of apples thinly sliced. Let it stand for two hours. Line a round sandwich tin with the kind of pastry you use for *flans*, and fill it with the mixture. A few blanched almonds should be dotted over the top, and the whole thing baked in a fairly hot oven for twenty minutes or so. The almonds and the spices give the tart a delicious and unexpected flavour. Cream should be served with it, and it is better eaten hot.

Here is a sweet, of which many of us read for the first time in a conciliatory scene in *The Constant Nymph*, a pleasant after-the-theatre concoction, Zambaglione, cousin to the French *Sabayon*.

Zambaglione

Eggs
Madeira or
Marsala
Sugar
Lemon

For eight people take six eggs, two glasses of Madeira or Marsala, nine ounces of castor sugar and the juice of a lemon. Whip the whites and put them with the rest of the ingredients into a thick saucepan. Cook this over a very slow heat—a methylated spirit stove is best—beating and stirring all the time. Do not let it boil, and do not stop stirring till it is really thick, when you and your adoring guests must eat it hot out of warmed glasses.

Fondue

Gruyère cheese
Eggs
Butter

Brillat-Savarin in his *Physiologie du Goût* tells of an amusing episode with a '*Fondue*', after which he gives the following recipe for this famous dish:

Take as many eggs as the number of guests demands, weigh them in their shells, and have ready some grated Gruyère cheese a third of the weight of the eggs and a piece of butter a sixth of their weight. Break the eggs into a casserole and beat them well together; then add the cheese and the butter. Put the casserole on a spirit stove and stir continuously till the mixture is thickened: add a little salt and a good deal of pepper, 'which', he says, 'is one of the definite characteristics of this ancient dish'. Serve on a lightly heated plate.

Onion Tart

Light pastry
Spring onions
Streaky bacon
Milk
Eggs

For those who have not tried it, an onion tart should most certainly be attempted at the earliest opportunity. Make an open tart of light pastry and cook it till lightly browned. Then fill it with the following mixture: three or four very thin rashers of streaky bacon fried very dry and broken in small pieces, some finely chopped spring onions browned in the bacon fat, half a pint of milk, four beaten eggs, salt and pepper, all mixed well together. Cook this slowly in the oven till it is firm and the top browned, and eat as quickly as possible.

IMPORTANT POINTS TO REMEMBER

1. In many of the recipes that follow, *simmering* will be mentioned. Remember that food will simmer just as well in the lower oven as on the simmering (right-hand) hot-plate. To use the lower oven for this purpose not only gives more space on the hot-plate, but, when the hot-plate is not in use, conserves the heat of the stove.

2. It is important to see that the hot-plate lids are always kept down when not in use. Do not keep kettles boiling on the hot-plate. You will only be wasting heat. Remember that the water in the Aga tank is nearly boiling, and will boil up in a minute or two.

3. A wipe in time saves nine. Keep the Aga top clean with a damp cloth as you use it.

> **N.B.**—The flues of the Aga Cooker should be cleaned quarterly (see page 20). Make a note to do so this month.

APRIL

THE FOOD OF THE MONTH

Food which is in season all the year round is given in the table on page 44.

Note.—Newcomers are printed in italics.

FISH

Bloaters	Dabs
Hake	Ling
Mackerel	Skate
Smelts	Whitebait

River Fish

Eels	Salmon
Trout	

Shell Fish

Crabs	Oysters
Scallops	

MEAT

Lamb	Pork

POULTRY

Ducklings	Guinea-fowl

GAME

Ortolans	Ptarmigan

VEGETABLES

Jerusalem Artichokes	
Asparagus	Horseradish
Parsnips	Radishes
Seakale	
Spanish Onions	
Spinach	
Spring Onions	
Watercress	

FRUIT

Rhubarb

EMPIRE IMPORTED FRESH FRUIT

Apples	
Avocado Pears	
Granadillas	Grapes
Grape Fruit	Limes
Melons	Oranges
Peaches	Pears
Persimmons	Plums
Pomegranates	
Quinces	

The following recipes are given during this month:

Young Carrot Soup

*Carrots
Onions
Bayleaf
Water
and possibly
Egg*

This is a Carrot Soup very suitable for April weather, if you like the flavour.

Scrape a pound of small carrots and put them into two and a half pints of water with two onions, a bayleaf, salt and pepper. Boil up and simmer for three or four hours. Sieve the carrots into another saucepan and strain the soup over them. Cook for a little longer, and serve, adding the yolk of an egg if you like.

Young Turnip Soup

And here is a young Turnip Soup. Cook in butter, but not long enough to brown them, six young turnips quartered. Add plenty of salt, a nice piece of butter and a pinch of sugar. Fill up with boiling water and simmer for four hours. When it is done, pass the turnips through a fine sieve and water them down with the liquid they have cooked in till the soup has the right consistency. Tiny cubes of fried toast with this, please, and you can enrich it if you like with an egg yolk beaten with a little cream.

Cheese Soup, I

*Consommé
Vegetables
Vermicelli
Cheese*

Cheese Soup in France is simply *consommé* into which the vegetables and spaghetti, macaroni or vermicelli have been added and cheese grated over, a kind of emasculated *Minestrone*.

Cheese Soup, II

*Onion
Milk
Water
Eggs
Cheese
French roll*

There is another kind of cheese soup which is worth trying. Fry a small finely chopped onion in an ounce of butter without browning it, then add a pint of milk and a pint of water. When this is nearly boiling, stir in two slightly beaten eggs, two ounces of grated cheese, and some salt and pepper. After adding the eggs and cheese you must not, of course, boil the soup, which on serving may be fortified by slices of French roll well dried in the oven.

APRIL

Eggs *sur le plat* with cheese and onions make a good dish for luncheon. They are usually served in small shallow individual dishes, or on a dish which will conveniently hold three or four eggs. On to one of these latter sprinkle a good tablespoonful of minced onion which has been cooked, but not browned, in butter. Break the eggs over this, sprinkle them with a little grated Parmesan cheese, and cook quickly in the oven until the eggs are set and the cheese slightly browned.

Eggs with
Cheese and
Onions

*Onions
Eggs
Cheese*

For a more substantial dish you will prefer this Spanish omelette, especially when spring onions, its crowning touch, are very young.

Fry in butter half a pound of thinly sliced new potatoes. When they are ready, add a quarter of a pound of finely chopped cooked ham. Season with cayenne pepper, or paprika, and a very little salt. Beat four eggs lightly, pour them over the potatoes and ham, and cook in the frying-pan till they are just set. Insert a slice under the omelette and turn the whole thing over on to a hot dish. Finally, and most important, sprinkle it with the finely chopped green part of a very young spring onion.

Spanish
Omelette

*New potatoes
Cooked ham
Cayenne or
Paprika
Eggs
Spring onion*

Although many will swear that there is nothing to beat Trout cooked *à la meunière* (and it is very hard to confute them), some will permit the addition of banana to this exquisite dish. Cook the trout as you would for *à la meunière*; that is, dip them in milk, roll them lightly in flour, season them and fry them in butter. Pour over the trout the butter in which they have cooked, flavoured with a good squeeze of lemon juice and some chopped parsley, and lay on each fish the long half of a small banana which you have meanwhile cooked in butter. Slices of button

Trout à la
Meunière
with
Bananas or
Mushrooms

*Trout
Butter
Lemon
Parsley
Bananas or
Mushrooms*

89

mushrooms tossed in butter can also be used as a garnish in place of the bananas.

Brandade of Salt Cod

Salt cod
Oil
Garlic
Milk

There is one famous dish of Salt Cod which I forgot to give last month. It is called *Brandade de Morue,* and although the salt cod we get in this country is not quite the same as the *morue* to which the title refers, we shall not go very far wrong in using it.

Flake a pound of cooked salt cod and keep the pieces hot. Have a saucepan ready with the sixth of a pint of oil and, when the oil is smoking, add the cod and a piece of crushed garlic the size of a pea and stir over the fire with a wooden spoon till the fish is well shredded. Keep on stirring and take the saucepan off the fire and, still stirring, add to the mixture, as you would for mayonnaise, about half a pint of oil, drop by drop. When the mixture gets too stiff, add now and then a tablespoonful of boiling milk. When the *brandade* is ready, it should be as thick as potato purée. See that it is well seasoned, and serve with *croûtons* of fried bread. This is a strong hint for Good Friday.

Fish Custard

Fillets of Fish
Fish stock
Egg
Milk
and possibly
Curry powder
and/or Onion
and/or
Bouquet garni

This is a Fish Custard which is handy for using up cold fish. But it is better to boil the fish especially for it, so that you can use the stock for the custard. Cook the trimmings of the fish in a pint of milk. Only half cook the fillets. Make a custard with this liquor and one egg, put the fillets into it, and bake in a tin of water for three-quarters of an hour. The custard can be improved by the addition of a little curry powder, and this in turn might be improved by boiling an onion with the fish trimmings. A *bouquet garni,* too, you will be able to suggest ... and so on. That is how great dishes are evolved.

APRIL

Fried Plaice
with
Anchovies

*Plaice
Hard-boiled eggs
Anchovies
Butter*

Something fried, for a change. Raise the fillets on one side of a small plaice without removing them, and crack the backbone at each end. Flour, egg-and-breadcrumb the fish and fry it in deep fat till golden. Now take out the backbone and stuff the cavity between the fillets with a mixture of the yolks of two eggs, hard boiled, four boned and pounded anchovies (or some anchovy essence) and two ounces of butter.

Hot Crab

*Crab
Mustard
Shallot
Parsley
Breadcrumbs
Butter
Cayenne pepper
Cream*

Crab comes in, and he can be eaten hot in the following simple manner. Chop the flesh as finely as possible and mix it in a bowl with a little plain mustard, in the proportion of a small teaspoonful to a large crab. Now mince a shallot and a little parsley and add it to the mixture with half as much fine breadcrumbs as there is crab. Meanwhile you should have melted about three ounces of butter. Pour this into the mixture of crab and breadcrumbs, stirring well till the *liaison* is complete, pepper it well (a little cayenne for those who like it hot in every sense of the word), and at the last add a little thick cream. Put this mixture back into the crab shells, or into separate *coquilles*, sprinkle with breadcrumbs, pour over a little melted butter, and cook in the oven—about five minutes—to brown.

Mushrooms
and Oysters

*Mushrooms
Oysters and
possibly Brown
or
Béchamel sauce*

Oysters might very well make their last appearance at our table this month in a fashion which hails from a country where they are never out of season. Simply cook some mushrooms in butter and poach an equal number of oysters lightly. Top each mushroom with an oyster and serve either plain on little pieces of buttered toast or with a brown or Béchamel sauce.

Mushrooms and Scallops

Mushrooms
Scallops
Béchamel sauce
Parsley

Large mushrooms can also be most appetisingly useful with scallops. Stew some scallops, chop up the white and red parts and keep them separate, bound very lightly with a little Béchamel sauce. Cook some large mushrooms in butter, and when they are done pile first the white, then the red part of the scallops on each of them. Serve very hot, with a final flourish to the colour scheme by a sprinkle of parsley.

Fried Scallops

Salad oil
Lemon
Parsley
Egg and breadcrumbs

Scallops can be fried, too. Marinate them for half an hour in a mixture of salad oil and lemon juice seasoned with salt and pepper. Turn them two or three times. Drain them, roll them in flour, egg-and-breadcrumb them, and fry them golden in boiling fat. Serve with fried parsley.

Spanish Beef Steak

Steak
Onion
Rice
Hard-boiled Egg
Gherkins
Breadcrumbs
Olive oil
Paprika

Here is a Spanish way of cooking beef steak.

Get a thick slice of steak, about a pound, and beat it out flat. Now spread on it a mixture of chopped onion, boiled rice, finely chopped hard-boiled egg, two chopped gherkins and a cupful of breadcrumbs previously soaked in olive oil. Season well, roll it up and tie it round, sprinkling the outside with flour and paprika. Melt some dripping in a baking-dish, put in the steak and bake for fifteen minutes in a hot oven, turning it over after the first five.

Fried Tripe

Tripe
Oil and vinegar
Egg and breadcrumbs
or Batter

Tripe-despisers should try fried tripe, which I first tasted at the Carlton Hotel, in London, not in Chorlton-on-the-Wiggle. (This remark is made not out of snobbishness, but as a recommendation of fried tripe!) It is extremely good, and is certain to convert them to frenzied tripe-eating, so long as they do not know what they are eating till after it is all over. Cut some well-cooked tripe into thinnish strips, and soak them for a little in a fifty-fifty marinade of oil and vinegar. Drain them, coat them with flour, and either egg-and-breadcrumb them or dip them in batter, and fry them to your appetite's content.

Liver, another 'offal', can be deliciously baked. It must be Calf's liver, and if you cook it in this way it will never turn out leathery, as it often does when fried. It will be more savoury too.

Baked Liver

Calf's liver
Streaky bacon
Parsley
Onion or Shallot
Butter

Fry the pieces of liver quickly in butter, so that each side is just browned. Chop together a rasher or two of streaky bacon, some parsley and an onion or, better, a shallot. Season and spread this mixture on the bottom of a flat fireproof dish. Place the slices of liver on this fragrant bed and anoint them with the butter in which the liver was fried. Cover with buttered greaseproof paper and bake in the oven for about a quarter of an hour. A simple, well-mashed (no lumps!) and not too buttery purée of potato is the perfect accompaniment to this exceptional dish.

If you want a fascinating way of serving chicken, here is one. It is quite easy, but needs great care.

Cassolettes of
Chicken

Potato purée
Cooked chicken
Mushrooms
Cream
Parsley

Make some purée of potato as for *croquettes*, and roll it into medium-sized balls. Shape these into the form of small drums, egg-and-breadcrumb them and fry them in boiling fat till they are golden brown. (Do not put in too many at once, or the temperature of the fat will drop.) Now carefully remove one end of each little drum, and even more carefully scoop out the inside. Then refill them with a delicately flavoured mixture of finely chopped cooked chicken and tossed mushrooms bound with a little cream.

Put the *cassolettes*, as they are called, back into the oven for a few minutes, and serve with fried parsley.

Cassoulet, however, is a very different matter. It is a kind of prolonged and elaborate stew of haricot beans, pork, goose, mutton, even partridges, hare, venison and heaven knows what, in the preparation of which many French towns and districts strive in gastronomic rivalry. There is even a *cassoulet* of Fish, too, but the one with which we are all familiar by now, though by another name, is our dear old friend, Pork and Beans. If you would care to try making it yourself, I am told that if you soak the haricot beans for twelve hours and next day put them in an earthenware *cassole*, or jar, with a piece of pickled pork, salt, pepper, two spoonfuls of treacle or sugar and a spoonful of made mustard, a covering of water and very slow cooking for twenty-four hours will produce the Right Thing.

After this lengthy process, Dumas' favourite method of cooking Haricot Beans seems simpler. That was to mix a pound of pickled pork cut in slices with a quart of soaked haricot beans, and to cover them with water and cook slowly till all the water was absorbed and the beans cooked. But, after all, this may turn out to take just as long, though I doubt it.

Pork figures again in our first Potato dish this month.

Peel some fairly large old potatoes, cut them in half lengthwise and scoop out a goodly hole in each half. Stuff this hole with sausagemeat to which you háve added some chopped parsley (and a little

Margin notes:
Pork and Beans

Haricot beans
Pickled pork
Treacle or Sugar
Mustard
Water

Haricot Beans

Stuffed Potatoes with Sausagemeat

Potatoes
Sausagemeat

APRIL

chopped garlic), and bake the potatoes with a tea-cupful of stock in a fireproof dish for about an hour, basting them pretty often. The oven should be a moderate one.

Parsley and possibly Garlic Stock

The usual Potato Cake of mashed potato cooked in a frying-pan with a plate over it is varied in Poland by the addition of a chopped hard-boiled egg and two chopped boned anchovies to each pound of potatoes. Or this mixture can be shaped into smaller cakes and fried in boiling fat.

Polish Potato Cake

Mashed potato Hard-boiled egg Anchovies

Spinach can be usefully combined with potatoes, by adding a purée of spinach with butter and cream to the usual potato purée. This might be very nice with the *cassolettes* described above.

Spinach and Potato Purée

We are familiar with baked apples and pears, but Baked Oranges are not so common on our tables. Just cut off the top of each orange, insert a little lemon juice mixed with sugar, put on the tops again and bake in a casserole with a little water and sugar. Whipped cream is suggested with this dish.

Baked Oranges

Oranges Lemon and possibly Whipped cream

A pleasant German pudding can be made with any kind of tinned fruit, or fresh fruit when it is in season. It is called *Kuchen*. You make an ordinary batter, as you would for Yorkshire Pudding, adding a little sugar and two tablespoonfuls of melted butter. Put it into a shallow fireproof dish and place over it pieces of the fruit you wish to use. Sprinkle with plenty of fine sugar and powdered cinnamon, and half a cupful of coarsely chopped walnuts. Bake in a moderate oven for three-quarters of an hour and serve with cream, custard or an appropriate sweet sauce.

Kuchen

Tinned fruit or Fresh fruit Batter Cinnamon Walnuts

Baked Pears
with
Chocolate
Sauce

Pears
Vanilla pod
Chocolate

Baked Pears are very delicious with chocolate sauce. Either bake the pears separately and pour a chocolate sauce over them before serving, both hot, of course; or prepare them in this way, which gives a more subtle flavour.

Cook some peeled, cored and quartered pears with a very little water, sugar and a vanilla pod. When they are nearly done, take them and the vanilla pod out, and melt in another saucepan some finely grated chocolate with a spoonful of the water in which the pears have been cooking. Pour this into the first saucepan, add a little butter and the pieces of pear, and sweeten a little more if you think it needs it. Continue cooking very slowly till the pears are quite done and the sauce creamy. Serve at once.

Orange
Jumbles

Almonds
Sugar
Butter
Flour
Oranges
Cochineal

A useful and delicious biscuit which can be served with cream or fruit is the Orange Jumble. To make these, shred a quarter of a pound of almonds and mix them with the same amount of white sugar, three ounces of butter, two ounces of flour and the grated rind and juice of two oranges. Mix this well together and colour with a drop or so of cochineal. Drop this mixture by teaspoonfuls on a greased baking-tin, and bake in a fairly slow oven till the biscuits are done. They should be set pretty widely apart in the tin, as each will spread out to about the size of a teacup rim. To say that they are indescribably charming really describes them.

Devilled
Biscuits

Butter
Chutney
Worcester
sauce
Water biscuits

The same discriminating source that supplied these adorable Jumbles also provides directions for Devilled Biscuits. Make a paste with a tablespoonful of butter, a teaspoonful of chutney and a dash of Worcester sauce. Spread this thinly on some very thin water biscuits, and put them into a hot oven for five minutes. A supply of radishes and cold cream-cheese provides the proper foil.

Bananas with cheese make a slightly heavier savoury. It is a combination which you will either like inordinately or detest. Try your luck, first, by eating a piece of cheese with your next banana. Here is the savoury.

Melt some butter, with salt and paprika, in an earthenware dish. Add a few peeled bananas halved lengthwise, sprinkle with breadcrumbs and grated Parmesan and Gruyère cheese, pour over a little melted butter, and cook in the oven till browned.

Bananas with Cheese

Butter
Paprika
Bananas
Breadcrumbs
Parmesan and Gruyère cheese

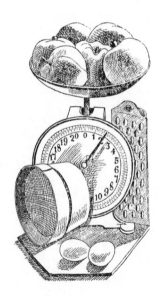

IMPORTANT POINTS TO REMEMBER

1. In many of the recipes that follow, *simmering* will be mentioned. Remember that food will simmer just as well in the lower oven as on the simmering (right-hand) hot-plate. To use the lower oven for this purpose not only gives more space on the hot-plate, but, when the hot-plate is not in use, conserves the heat of the stove.
2. It is important to see that the hot-plate lids are always kept down when not in use. Do not keep kettles boiling on the hot-plate. You will only be wasting heat. Remember that the water in the Aga tank is nearly boiling, and will boil up in a minute or two.
3. A wipe in time saves nine. Keep the Aga top clean with a damp cloth as you use it.

N.B.—Drain off a pint of water from the bottom tap quarterly. This will prevent sediment accumulating in the bottom of the tank. Make a note to do so this month.

MAY

THE FOOD OF THE MONTH

Food which is in season all the year round is given in the table on page 44.

Note.—Newcomers are printed in italics.

FISH

Sea Fish

Hake	*Herrings*
Mackerel	Smelts
Whitebait	

River Fish

Eels	Salmon
Trout	

Shell Fish

Crabs	Scallops

MEAT

Lamb

POULTRY

Ducklings
Guinea-fowl

GAME

Ortolans

VEGETABLES

Jerusalem Artichokes
Asparagus *Green Corn*
Green Peas Horseradish
Parsnips *New Potatoes*
Seakale
Spanish Onions
Spinach
Spring Onions
Watercress

FRUIT

Green Gooseberries
Rhubarb

EMPIRE IMPORTED FRESH FRUIT

Apples
Avocado Pears
Granadillas Grapes
Grape Fruit Limes
Melons Peaches
Persimmons Pears
Pomegranates
Quinces

The following recipes are given during this month:

Fish
Chowder

Cod or Haddock
Fat salt pork
Onion
Potatoes
Milk

If geography forbids us Clam Chowder, we can make a Fish Chowder instead.

Buy a small cod or haddock weighing about four pounds. Skin the fish, bone it, and cut the flesh into pieces about two inches square. Bring two cupfuls of water to the boil and cook in this the cod's head, tail and bones for twenty minutes. While this is cooking, cut a one-and-a-half-inch cube of fat salt pork into small pieces, extract the fat by frying and cook a sliced onion in the fat for five minutes. Now strain the fat into a stewpan, add to it four cupfuls of potatoes cut into three-quarter-inch cubes which have been boiled in enough water to cover them for five minutes and then drained. Add to the fat and potatoes two cupfuls of water and cook for five minutes. Now pour in the liquor from the bones and put in the pieces of fish. Cover and simmer for ten minutes, when you add four cupfuls of scalded milk, a tablespoonful of salt, an eighth of a tablespoonful of pepper and three tablespoonfuls of butter. Bring to the boil, simmer a little longer and serve.

The unfamiliar aspect of this recipe is due to its being a transcription from an American one.

Spring
Vegetable
Soup

Carrots
Turnips
Leeks
Cabbage
Lettuce
Peas
Chervil

Now is the time for a Spring Vegetable Soup.

Scrape some young carrots and turnips and cut them in thin slices, also the white part of two leeks treated in the same way, and the heart of a young cabbage cut in four. Cook these slowly in butter in a covered saucepan till they are tender. Then add a quartered lettuce heart, a handful of fresh peas and a little chervil chopped up, and finally enough stock to serve your purpose when the soup has been reduced by a third. Just before you are ready for it —practically on its way from the saucepan to the tureen—mix well in with it the beaten yolk of an egg.

Stock
Egg

Lettuce Soup is equally spring-like, but much easier.

Cut two lettuces and a handful of spinach into strips, and cook them in butter with a handful of parsley coarsely chopped, till they are all quite soft. Add hot water, salt and pepper, bring to the boil and simmer for about three-quarters of an hour. Before serving add a beaten yolk of an egg to this soup too, and be sure that the parsley stalks, and the hard parts of the lettuce and spinach leaves, have been discarded, or the soup will be stringy.

Lettuce Soup
Lettuces
Spinach
Parsley
Water
Egg

We can still bake some potatoes in their jackets, so let us do so now, with a little difference. Cut off a piece of their ends, scoop out their insides and make a smooth purée of it, adding a little grated cheese, if you like. Half fill each case with this, break an egg into each, moisten with a drop of cream and bake in the oven till the eggs are set.

Eggs in
Potatoes

*Potatoes and
possibly Cheese
Egg
Cream*

Omelettes are excellent in May, and indeed in most other months. Two suggestions for this one are to fill your omelette either with pieces of artichoke bottoms or red pimentoes warmed in butter. It is pleasant sometimes to have something out of season, and both these vegetables are almost as good in tins as they are out of the greengrocer's, if indeed he has them.

Omelette
aux fonds
d'artichauts
or aux piments

It is Empire month, when we are urged to buy Empire goods more lavishly than in the rest of the year. Empire Salmon is one of these. No one will claim for it the admirable flavour of our own river

Salmon
à la Mornay

*Salmon
Onion*

Fish stock
or Water
Bouquet garni
Cheese
Cream
Lemon

fish, but it can be made extremely eatable if it is treated properly. One suggestion for its presentation at the most particular table is Salmon *à la Mornay*.

Brown your slices of salmon quickly with a chopped onion in an ounce of butter. Add three-quarters of a pint of fish stock (or water, if you have no stock ready), salt, pepper, and a *bouquet* of parsley, thyme and bayleaf. Cover and simmer for about twenty minutes. When the fish is nearly done, cook a heaped tablespoonful of flour in an ounce of butter for five minutes in another pan, take out the fish and keep it warm, and make a sauce with the butter, flour and the strained liquor in which the salmon has been cooked. Bring it to the boil, simmer, and add a tablespoonful of grated Parmesan cheese, a little cream and a good squeeze of lemon juice. Season, pour over the fish, glaze if you like in the oven, and serve.

Stuffed
Herrings, I

Herrings
Parsley
Breadcrumbs
Butter
Egg
Milk

This is a way of Stuffing Herrings which is not very well known. It deserves better acquaintance.

Split open some large herrings with soft roes, which you will remove and chop up with parsley and soft breadcrumbs. Mix well together and season with a little pepper. Now melt some butter—not too much—in a saucepan, break into it an egg, stir it, add the mixture of chopped roes, stir again so that it does not set before all is well mixed. Remove the backbones of the herrings as best you can, stuff the fish with the egg and roe, and bake them in a fireproof dish with a little butter for nearly half an hour. They should be served with a sauce of the liquor in which they have baked stirred over the fire for a few minutes with a little milk.

This is another way of stuffing them.

Split them and remove their backbones. Season them with pepper and salt and spread on the inside a thin layer of forcemeat composed of one part finely chopped suet to two parts breadcrumbs, some chopped parsley and a little grated lemon rind, all mixed together and moistened with milk. Roll up the herrings from neck to tail (you should, by the way, have removed their heads and tail fins), tie or skewer each of them, pack them tightly in a buttered pie-dish, cover with buttered paper, and bake in a moderate oven for about an hour, not less.

Oranges add a special distinction to the fish course. For example, Sole or Red Mullet *à la meunière à l'orange*, especially the Red Mullet.

Having floured the fish and fried it in butter, dish it and lay on it a row of orange sections carefully peeled and with the pips and pith removed. Warm them through, squeeze a little orange juice into the butter in which the fish was cooked, brown it lightly and pour it over. If a stronger orange taste (which I advocate) is desired, a few very thin *julienne* strips of orange peel, boiled for a few minutes to remove their bitterness, can also be added.

Sole *à l'hongroise* is a simple dish and admirable for the warmer weather.

Fry in butter, without browning, a dessertspoonful of chopped onion lightly seasoned with paprika. Add three tablespoonfuls of white wine, a small cupful of fish stock (which you will have made from the trimmings of the sole) and two small tomatoes peeled and roughly chopped. Cook this together for about ten minutes. Meanwhile arrange the fillets in a buttered dish; now pour over the mixture and cook

Stuffed
Herrings, II

Herrings
Suet
Breadcrumbs
Parsley
Lemon
Milk

Sole
Red Mullet
à la meunière
à l'orange

Sole or
Red Mullet
Oranges

Sole à
l'hongroise

Onion
Paprika
White wine
Fish stock
Tomatoes
Sole
Cream
Lemon

in a moderate oven till done. Take out the fillets and keep them warm, reduce the liquid in which they have been cooked till it is thick, then add a little cream and a squeeze of lemon, and pour it over them.

Lobster
Pancakes, I

Pancakes
Lobster
Paprika
Béchamel sauce
Tomato purée
Cheese

Lobster Pancakes are seasonable, too, and out of the ordinary.

Make some pancakes as thin as possible, using unsweetened batter, of course, and keep them warm. Toss some pieces of cooked lobster, cut fairly small, in butter; season them with paprika, and bind them with a little thick Béchamel sauce to which you have added a spoonful of tomato purée. Stuff the pancakes with this, arrange them on a long fireproof dish, cover with more Béchamel sauce, sprinkle with grated cheese and brown quickly before serving.

Lobster
Pancakes, II

Pancakes
Lobster
Mushrooms
Tomatoes
Truffle
Brandy
Cream

A more elaborate stuffing can be prepared by making a sauce to bind the pieces of lobster out of a few slices of mushrooms and tomatoes cooked in butter, a sliced truffle and the red part of the lobster all chopped together and mixed with a little brandy and some cream. But in this case, do not sprinkle with cheese or brown the sauce.

Fricassée of
Scallops

Scallops
Béchamel sauce
Lemon
Egg
Parsley

Those first-cousins of the lobster, Scallops, make an excellent *fricassée*, if we cannot rise to a lobster. Cut the scallops in four pieces and stew them in a good white sauce for about three-quarters of an hour. A squeeze of lemon juice, the beaten yolk of an egg, and a very little chopped parsley should be stirred in at the last moment. It makes a very pretty dish, which you might well adorn with a few delicate little heaps of peas.

Beef in Lettuce Leaves, I

The more frequent appearance of lettuces in the shop windows should remind us of a dish which is not very often encountered in this country, though it is popular in various forms on the Continent and in the Near East, whence I fancy it hails. *Beef Rice Egg Milk Lettuce Stock*

This is Beef (or other meat) in Lettuce Leaves. There are many ways of preparing this. I will give two.

For the first mince a pound of raw beef, and boil a gill of rice in milk. Let the rice get cold. Beat up an egg in a little milk and add it to the rice and beef, with some pepper and salt. Take a good spoonful of the mixture and wrap it in a lettuce leaf, repeating this till you have used it all. Tie the lettuce leaves with cotton and brown them all over in butter. Cover with some good, well-flavoured stock and cook very slowly in the oven for two hours.

For the second way you will want the same quantity of minced beef. Mix it with a tablespoonful of finely chopped onion, two ounces of chopped suet, a pinch of allspice, salt and pepper. Shape the mixture into pieces about the size of a small egg. Wrap each piece in a lettuce leaf, and arrange them as closely as possible in a long fireproof dish. Cover them with stock or gravy, with a piece of buttered paper, and the lid, and cook for about half an hour. Beef in Lettuce Leaves, II *Beef Onion Suet Allspice Lettuce Stock or Gravy*

Young cabbage leaves may be used instead of lettuce so long as they are first boiled for five minutes; or the stuffed leaves can be braised on a bed of bacon-rind, sliced carrots and onions, and a *bouquet* of parsley, thyme and bayleaf. This last is specially recommended.

Inventiveness can also be exercised in the concoction of various savoury stuffings of veal, Veal or Chicken in

Lettuce
Leaves

Onion
Chicken or
Veal
Breadcrumbs
Stock
Egg
Lettuce
Tomato sauce

chicken, and so on. The Americans, for instance, have a version of this dish in which the stuffing consists of half a tablespoonful of lightly fried chopped onion, a cupful of chopped cooked chicken or veal, the same of fine white breadcrumbs moistened with stock and a beaten egg, salt and pepper. They serve this kind of lettuce roll with a tomato sauce poured round it.

Veal Cutlets
with
Cucumber

Veal
Butter
Cream
Paprika
Cucumber

Cucumbers must be mentioned here, not so much for themselves as for a summery amalgamation with veal. Cook some thin *escalopes* in butter, and to the butter and veal juices add, after the cutlets have been removed, a good cupful of cream, salt and pepper and a pinch of paprika. Stir this all well together and boil quickly for a few minutes till it thickens, and then add a few pieces of butter off the flame. Now pour this over the veal which you have surrounded with rounds of boiled cucumber. A really marvellous combination of contrasting flavours.

Swedish
Lamb Cutlets

Lamb cutlets
Onions
Shallots
Parsley
Thyme
Bayleaf
Lemon
Oil
Butter
Breadcrumbs
Apples
White wine
Horseradish

When you are tired of all the usual ways of presenting Lamb Cutlets, the Swedish fashion may appeal to you.

Sprinkle the cutlets with minced onions and shallots, parsley, thyme and bayleaf, the juice of a lemon and a few drops of oil. Marinade them thus for half an hour, turning them once or twice. Then dry them, brush them over with melted butter, and grill them.

Meanwhile you have peeled and sliced half a pound of apples and stewed them quickly to a purée with a little white wine (the wine could be omitted). Just before dishing up, stir into this purée two good tablespoonfuls of grated horseradish. Pour it into the centre of the dish and serve the cutlets round it.

MAY

There is a good deal to be said for the French method of roasting a joint of lamb, which is to do so on a bed of sliced potatoes, onions and carrots well mixed together. The disadvantage is that all your dripping is absorbed by the vegetables, but they are very delicious, and this way of cooking imparts an entrancing flavour to the cold meat. Garlic is also added in most parts of France, either inserted near the bone, or a little chopped very finely and put in the bottom of the dish. I am told that the after effects of the latter method are less potent!

Roast Lamb
French fashion

Lamb
Potatoes
Onions
Carrots
and possibly
Garlic

An alternative recipe to the Veal with cucumber is an Austrian dish called *Kahab*, a different form of a *sauté*.

Cut about a pound of veal cutlet into pieces about the size of a matchbox. Put a good piece of butter into an earthenware casserole or stewpan, melt it and add the meat seasoned with salt and pepper, a quarter of a teaspoonful of caraway seeds (in a muslin bag), a very small onion and half a lemon both very thinly sliced. Fry all this for about ten minutes, not too fast, then add half a pint of sour cream, put on the lid and cook slowly in a moderate oven for about three-quarters of an hour.

Kahab
(Sauté of Veal)

Veal Cutlet
Caraway seeds
Onion
Lemon
Sour cream

A *Fritto Misto* of Fruit was suggested for January, or indeed for any other month. The orthodox *Fritto Misto* of Meat consists of all or any of the following: veal cutlet, calf's liver, calf or lamb sweetbread, veal or sheep's kidney, an aubergine or artichoke, brains, and a cauliflower. The latter must, of course, be parboiled. All these ingredients you cut into thin slices (the cauliflower into flowerets), season them and dip them in melted butter and flour. They should then be *sauté-d* in separate pans

Fritto Misto
of Meat

Veal cutlet
Calf's liver
Calf or Lamb
sweetbread
Veal or Sheep's
kidney
Aubergine or
Artichoke
Brains

Cauliflower
Lemon

in plenty of butter, the juice of a lemon squeezed into the mingled butter after they are cooked, and this sauce poured over the pieces, which should be served very hot. Or, if it is preferred, they can all be fried very crisply in oil. In any case, the dish should be garnished with lemons.

American
Fried Chicken

Chicken
Pork fat
and possibly
Milk and Cream

We have discussed Spring Chicken already, but not in a fried fashion. This is a way they have of cooking him in the Southern States of America. It is perfectly simple, as you would expect, but very good indeed.

Cut a young chicken in pieces, wash them in cold water, drain them, but do not wipe them dry. Now sprinkle them with salt and pepper and coat them as thickly as possible with flour, pressing it well on. Then fry them in plenty of salt pork fat till they are well browned and tender. They are usually served with a plain white sauce made of half milk and half cream.

American
Baked
Chicken

Chicken
Egg and
breadcrumbs

Another American way of cooking chicken is to cut it up in pieces which are then salted and peppered and rolled in egg and breadcrumbs. Do not fry them, but put them in a well-greased baking-dish and bake them for half an hour in a hot oven. After they have been cooking for five minutes they should be basted with melted butter. A white sauce is also served with these.

Vol-au-vent

Vol-au-vent cases can be bought from most pastry-cooks, if you do not want to take the trouble of making them yourself. As a matter of fact, for the ordinary cook, these are one of the few things which are better bought. They are, in any case, extremely useful, for a most attractive course can always be prepared with their help. Any kind of white meat, cut into small pieces and combined with mushrooms or other meats such as ham and tongue in a delicate sauce can be used for fillings, as can cold pieces of fish or shellfish bound with an appropriate sauce. Put them in the oven with their savoury contents and put on the little top a trifle jauntily, for the *vol-au-vent*, as its name betrays, is a slightly frivolous form of food.

Your own ingenuity will devise various fillings. Here are one or two for your guidance.

First, with chicken: that is small cubes of cooked chicken and ham or tongue, slices of mushrooms (the little bottled ones are best for this), and truffles, all mixed with a thick Béchamel sauce, flavoured with salt, pepper and aromatic spice.

Chicken
Vol-au-vent
Cooked
Chicken
Ham
or Tongue
Mushrooms
Truffles
Béchamel sauce
Aromatic spice

Second, with vegetables: for instance, a mixture of cooked cauliflower and grated cheese and a good cream or mushroom sauce.

Vegetable
Vol-au-vent
Cooked
cauliflower
Cheese
Cream sauce or
Mushroom
sauce

Third, more for curiosity's sake, because the *Vol-au-vent à la financière* is the one most commonly served in restaurants, though I doubt if the ingredients are always correctly used: truffles cooked in Madeira, a brown sauce made with good stock, little pieces of mushrooms, *fonds d'artichauts, quenelles*, and to give it some substance, however airy, little bits of sweetbread cooked in butter.

Vol-au-vent à
la financière

Asparagus cannot always be eaten plainly, however much we may be addicted to it; but if it is, we might take a tip from the Belgians. It is often heartbreaking for many of us to have to leave the delicious melted butter on our plates after we have sucked the last fragrant drops from the asparagus. A

Asparagus
Butter with
Egg

sensible Flemish custom is to serve each guest with half the hot yolk of a hard-boiled egg, which is then crushed and used with the butter. Or the egg and butter can be mixed beforehand—in the proportion of half an egg yolk to two tablespoonfuls of butter —seasoned and served with the asparagus.

Asparagus à la Polonaise

Asparagus
Hard-boiled egg
Parsley
Breadcrumbs

The Polish garnish which we have encountered with *petits poussins* is well adapted to asparagus. After you have dished the asparagus, well drained, sprinkle the tips with hot hard-boiled egg yolk and finely chopped parsley, and throw over it at the last moment some fresh breadcrumbs which have been made golden in butter when it is just foaming.

Mushrooms stuffed with Fish

Mushrooms
Parsley
Garlic or Onion
Cold fish
Egg
Breadcrumbs

Mushrooms stuffed with fish are a good savoury or luncheon dish. Lightly fry as many mushrooms as you want (they should be fairly large, but not too coarse), and heap upon them a mixture of their stalks chopped up and tossed in butter, some parsley, a tiny bit of garlic (or onion) and the remains of any cold fish you have by you, all mixed together and bound with the yolk of an egg. Sprinkle with breadcrumbs, dot with butter and bake for about a quarter of an hour. Serve on toast or fried bread.

Potatoes with Lemon

New potatoes
Lemon
Butter
Parsley

Imported new potatoes do not taste much, so we can make this experiment with them. Half cook some small new potatoes, and pour the water away, except just enough to cover them. Into this squeeze the juice of a lemon and finish cooking. Drain them well, and pour over melted butter, sprinkling them as they leave the kitchen with chopped parsley.

Granadilla or Passion Fruit Cream

Pomegranates have already reminded us of Empire sweets. Granadilla Cream is another unusual flavour which should become popular. As far as I can gather, Granadillas and Passion Fruit are to all intents and purposes the same. They both come from South Africa, and Australia too, and the pulp is imported in tins. You may prefer to rub the pulp through a sieve again, as it is populated by little black seeds which, however decorative they are, may not invariably meet with favour.

Granadilla pulp
Sugar
Lemon
Cream
Gelatine

To make the Cream, add to the pulp, sieved or not, a tablespoonful of fine sugar and a teaspoonful of lemon juice, and let it stand in a covered basin for about three-quarters of an hour. Stiffly whip up half a pint of cream, fold it lightly into the pulp, then stir in two ounces of gelatine which you have dissolved in a little hot water. Mould it and let it get cool, and serve iced, if possible.

The Granadilla pulp gives an additional and pleasant flavour to fruit salads, and by the way, do not forget also to order a tin of Golden Berries, which are our old friends, the Cape Gooseberries (once in their dried state so universally, and unfortunately, decorative) masquerading charmingly as an eatable.

Golden Berries

Canada gives us Lemon Pie. All the really lovable old Mommas on the Pictures make a pie of some kind, and I am sure that Lemon Pie is a favourite !

Lemon Pie

Make a *flan* case of puff pastry, baking till three-quarters done. Meanwhile mix a dessertspoonful of cornflour with a little milk till it is smooth, boil a pint of milk and pour it over the cornflour, stirring well. Now add an ounce of sugar, the finely grated rind of a lemon and the yolks of three eggs, and stir on a low heat till the mixture thickens. Pour this into the *flan* case. Beat the egg whites as stiffly as possible, stir six ounces of castor sugar lightly into

Pastry
Cornflour
Milk
Lemon
Eggs

the froth and spread it on top of the pie, which you will now bake in a moderate oven till the méringue is crisp and golden.

Some Momma!

Devils on
Horseback, I

Bacon
French plums
Almonds
Paprika and
Cayenne

Devils on
Horseback, II

Bacon
Chicken's liver
Onion
Parsley
Cayenne

The Angels having flown with the oysters, Devils on Horseback are now the order of the day. These are our tiny friends, the thin rolls of bacon, each stuffed with a stoned French plum in which has been inserted a peeled Jordan almond tossed in butter and seasoned with salt, paprika and cayenne. A different Devil is a stuffing of a good piece of chicken's liver sprinkled with finely chopped onion and parsley, salt, pepper, and cayenne. Tie or skewer the little rolls, and bake them in the oven. Serve on toast, very hot.

These little rolls are often a godsend—like the *vol-au-vent*—for they can be filled with all kinds of stuffings, and have been known to tempt the most difficult palate even in the dog-days.

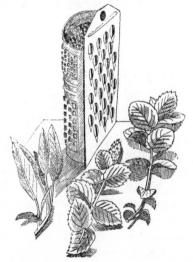

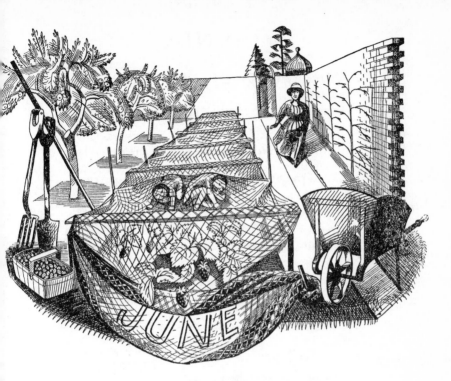

IMPORTANT POINTS TO REMEMBER

1. In many of the recipes that follow, *simmering* will be mentioned. Remember that food will simmer just as well in the lower oven as on the simmering (right-hand) hot-plate. To use the lower oven for this purpose not only gives more space on the hot-plate, but, when the hot-plate is not in use, conserves the heat of the stove.

2. It is important to see that the hot-plate lids are always kept down when not in use. Do not keep kettles boiling on the hot-plate. You will only be wasting heat. Remember that the water in the Aga tank is nearly boiling, and will boil up in a minute or two.

3. A wipe in time saves nine. Keep the Aga top clean with a damp cloth as you use it.

JUNE

THE FOOD OF THE MONTH

Food which is in season all the year round is given in the table on page 44.

Note.—Newcomers are printed in italics.

FISH

Sea Fish

Hake	Herrings
Mackerel	Whitebait

River Fish

Eels	Salmon
	Trout

Shell Fish

Crabs	Scallops

MEAT

Lamb

POULTRY

Ducklings   Guinea-fowl

GAME

Buck Venison

VEGETABLES

Jerusalem Artichokes
Asparagus   *Aubergine*
Cauliflower   Green Corn
Green Peas   Horseradish
New Potatoes   Seakale
Spinach
Spring Onions
Watercress

FRUIT

Apricots   *Cherries*
Green Gooseberries
Melons   *Raspberries*
Strawberries

EMPIRE
IMPORTED
FRESH FRUIT

Apples	Granadillas
Grapes	Grape Fruit
Limes	Naartjes
Oranges	Pears

The following recipes are given during this month:

Cucumber Soup

Cucumbers
Vinegar
Butter
White stock
Breadcrumbs
Milk
Onions
Sugar
Cream

Cucumber Soup makes a very good introduction to a June dinner.

Peel two cucumbers, cut them into small pieces, remove the seeds, and boil the pieces for three minutes in some water to which you have added a dash of vinegar. Drain them well and put them into a saucepan with four ounces of butter. When that has melted, add two pints of white stock, a coffee-cupful of fine white breadcrumbs soaked in milk, two onions cut up small, salt, and a pinch of sugar. Bring this to the boil, simmer a little while, stirring occasionally. Strain the soup when it is done, and just before serving stir in four or five, or more, tablespoonfuls of cream.

Spanish Omelette, II

Potato
Tomato
Onion
Pimento
and possibly
Parsley

A different Spanish Omelette from that which I described in April can be made as follows:

Cut a potato in small cubes and fry in butter. In a separate pan fry also in butter a peeled tomato, an onion and a red pepper (pimento) finely chopped. Pour your omelette mixture into the pan, add these ingredients, season all fairly highly, and cook the omelette like a pancake, tossing it once. Serve flat, with a sprinkling of parsley if you like.

Œufs mollets

Œufs mollets, or peeled soft-boiled eggs, make a welcome change for summer meals. They take six minutes, no more, to cook from the time the water in which they have been plunged has come to the boil again. They should then be left for a minute or two in cold water and carefully shelled. They can be kept warm, if desired, in moderately salted hot water.

Various ways of serving them will at once occur to you. For instance, all the garnishes for poached

eggs (spinach, asparagus tips or purée, endives, peas
à la française) can equally well be applied to them, or
they can be coated with various sauces, Soubise,
Béchamel, Mornay, Tomato, Robert, and so on. In
hot weather they certainly have a less forbidding appearance than poached eggs, and there is always the
element of surprise about them for the uninitiated.

A *Fritto Misto* of Fish is our last variation on this
theme.

Any small fish could be used to compile a very
charming gastronomic comment on a warm mid-
day or evening: very small slip soles or other little
flat fish, tiny whiting, prawns, pieces of lobster,
whitebait—all these and others could be employed to
assemble a light summer dish which, after its ingredients have been rolled in egg and breadcrumbs
and fried, should certainly be accompanied by some
beautifully green fried parsley.

Before Mackerel and Green Gooseberries both
disappear, we should eat them in conjunction.

Cut the mackerel in three, crosswise, and boil
them in a *court-bouillon* of wine or vinegar, to which
you have added a pinch of fennel if you can get it.
(Don't be discouraged by this instruction, for the
fish can also be boiled in water and vinegar, though
they will, of course, then lack the finer flavour
which the *court-bouillon* imparts.) Drain the pieces
and skin them, and serve them with a sauce made
by cooking a pound of green gooseberries with
three ounces of sugar in just enough water to cover
them. When the fruit is done, rub through a hair
sieve, and add this new combination of flavours to
your gastronomic repertoire.

Marginal notes:

Fritto of Misto
Fish

Any small fish

Mackerel
with
Gooseberry
Sauce

*Mackerel
White wine
or Vinegar
Fennel
Gooseberries
Sugar*

JUNE

Sole Villeroi

*Mushrooms
Parsley
Shallots or
Onions
Fillets of Sole
Milk
Cream
Fish stock
Breadcrumbs*

Sole *Villeroi* is more suitable for a special occasion.

Toss in an ounce of butter half a dozen mushrooms finely chopped, a tablespoonful of chopped parsley and two of minced shallots or onions. When they are cooked, let them get cold. Have some fillets of sole ready, spread some of the mixture on each, roll them up, tie with cotton, arrange in a buttered *sauté* pan and cook for ten minutes. Now have some little china cases ready, and into each put a rolled fillet with a small mushroom on top, filling up the case with a good white sauce made with milk, cream, and a little fish stock made from the trimmings of the sole. Sprinkle each with a few breadcrumbs, and brown quickly in the oven.

Anchovy Cream of Turbot

*Turbot
Breadcrumbs
Milk
Worcester sauce
Ground mace
Cayenne
Cream
Eggs
Peas
Cream sauce
Anchovy
essence*

Anchovy Cream of Turbot is a decorative dish for a dinner-party.

Pass a pound of turbot through a sieve, and mix it with a teaspoonful of breadcrumbs soaked in milk and well drained, half a teaspoonful of Worcester sauce, the same of salt, a pinch of ground mace, a sprinkle of cayenne, and a cupful of good cream. Whip up the whites of four eggs and fold them into this mixture. Pour it into a buttered *soufflé* mould and cook for twenty minutes. Serve surrounded with green peas and covered with a rich cream sauce well flavoured with anchovy essence.

Lobster à la Newburg, I

*Lobster
Madeira
Cream
Egg
Rice*

The horrors of cutting up live lobsters to make Lobster *à la Newburg* are avoided by this simple method, which gives very satisfactory results.

Chop up the meat of a medium-sized lobster, and fry it in an ounce of butter in a stewpan, seasoning it well. Then add enough Madeira nearly to cover the pieces, and let it reduce almost entirely. Add to

this half a pint of cream and a beaten egg yolk, and
let it thicken. Serve very hot with a little rice.

A simpler way, without the use of wine, is to
warm up the pieces of lobster in butter, and to add
to them a mixture of two egg yolks, half a gill of
thick cream, a few drops of onion juice, a saltspoonful of salt, the same of Krona pepper and a
trifle of nutmeg. Stir till the mixture thickens, and
serve at once.

*Lobster à la
Newburg, II*

*Lobster
Eggs
Cream
Onion juice
Krona pepper
Nutmeg*

A remarkable dish can be prepared from Beef
and New Peas. Like so many really first-class dishes,
it is extremely easy to make.

*Beef Braised
with New Peas*

*Steak
Peas*

Take a nice piece of steak, salt and pepper it and
brown it in butter in a casserole for about ten
minutes, turning it so that the meat is 'closed' all
over. Now just add some fresh-shelled peas (they
should be all about the same size, and the smaller
the better), a little more salt and pepper, put on the
lid and simmer very gently for two and a half or
three hours. As a result of this masterly inattention
you will obtain a marvellous mixture of beef, butter
and peas, the exquisite flavours of each having
entered into the other. And don't, by the way, begrudge the beef, which is very eatable indeed when
cold.

I have already advocated Roast Lamb *à la française.*
To cook the joint *en cocotte* is also a pleasing method.
Put it in the *cocotte* with some lightly fried young
carrots and turnips, a few button onions and a
couple of glasses of dry white wine. Or stock can be
used by those who do not like the taste of wine.
When the joint is cooked, add a little cream and
chopped parsley to the gravy before serving.

*Lamb
en cocotte*

*Lamb
Carrots
Turnips
Onions
White wine
or Stock
Cream
Parsley*

Veal Cutlets with Turnips An unusual way of serving veal cutlets is to egg-and-breadcrumb and fry them, and dish them up round a fine purée of turnips.

Veal Kidney Veal Kidney makes an admirable dish, and is often liked by those who find the flavour of sheep's kidney too strong. It can be cooked in many ways, sliced or whole; plainly with butter in a casserole; in the same way with the addition of *fines herbes*; with pieces of blanched bacon, mushrooms and tiny onions. When it is plainly cooked it can with advantage be served with a dryish purée of tomatoes and with tomatoes stuffed with forcemeat or *petits pois* surrounding it.

Veal Kidney à la Liègoise

Veal kidney
Gin
Juniper berries

But the best way of all, to my thinking, is to cook it whole in butter in a casserole, and just before serving to throw in a wineglassful of burnt gin and a few crushed juniper berries. This is quite wonderful, and if you can get the berries fresh from your own or a friend's garden, so much the better. Otherwise they can be obtained in bottles, but they should be well crushed.

Chicken Bonne Femme

Chicken
Pickled pork
Potatoes
and possibly
Veal gravy

The following is a very simple but most exquisite fashion of cooking a chicken, preferably a spring chicken. Blanch, by boiling for a few minutes, two or three slices of breast of pickled pork. Cut them in pieces and fry them in a little butter. Take them out and fry the chicken all over in the same fat. Having done this, put it into a cocotte with the pieces of pork and the fat in which it has been fried: but first you will have fried lightly in that fat about three-quarters of a pound of potatoes cut into not too thin rounds. Put these round the chicken, cover

the cocotte and cook in the oven for about an hour.
Serve in the cocotte. The addition of a few tablespoonfuls of veal gravy at the end is a pleasant, but
not absolutely necessary, extra.

Here are three ways of serving asparagus.

One. Cook some asparagus tips and drain them
well. Melt a piece of butter in a saucepan, add a
cupful of cream, salt, pepper and a grating of nutmeg. Mix well together till boiling, add the asparagus tips, and cook on till the cream reduces and
thickens.

Asparagus à la
Crème

*Asparagus
Cream
Nutmeg*

Two. Cook the asparagus, drain it and dish it up
flat. Coat the heads with a little Mornay sauce,
sprinkle with a little grated Parmesan cheese, cover
the stalks with buttered paper and brown the heads
quickly.

Asparagus au
Gratin

*Asparagus
Mornay sauce
Parmesan*

Three. This is rather a novelty. Cook the asparagus till nearly done. Cut off the tips, not too shortly,
and put them into cold water. Drain them and let
them dry. Now roll them in flour and tie a few together in little bundles. Dip these in beaten egg and
fry in deep fat till golden. The small thin asparagus
(sprew) is perhaps best for this dish.

Asparagus
Fritters

*Asparagus
Egg*

An Italian recipe for serving Cauliflower will be
appreciated by those who are rather tired of the
everlasting cauliflower with plain white sauce.

Fry a small onion and two boned anchovies
chopped very fine in some butter. Add to this half
a pint of stock, a teaspoonful of mixed herbs, and a
dash of vinegar, thickening with a little flour if you
wish. Pour this unusual sauce over the boiled or
steamed cauliflower.

Cauliflower
Italian fashion

*Onion
Anchovies
Stock
Mixed herbs
Vinegar
Cauliflower*

JUNE

Strawberries
au Kirsch

*Strawberries
Cream
Kirsch*

There are those who swear by Strawberries *au Kirsch* as their happiest summer experience. We can but try them. Cut a pound of strawberries in halves. Whip up some cream with sugar, adding a liqueur-glassful of Kirsch, and half a dozen or so squashed strawberries to give it colour. Sprinkle the strawberries with sugar and mix them well with the cream. Curaçao or Grand Marnier could be used instead of Kirsch, if preferred, and a good dash of any of these liqueurs to ordinary strawberries and cream has many devotees.

Strawberries
with Orange,
I

*Strawberries
Oranges*

And if the weather is wet, and the berries look a little dishevelled for a proper appearance at dessert, do not let us despise the help of an orange or two by mixing the juice of two of them with a purée made by passing a pound of strawberries through a hair sieve and adding the requisite amount of sugar. This purée makes a regal bed for the more presentable berries which you have, of course, put aside.

Strawberries
with Orange,
II

*Strawberries
Oranges
Cherries
Maraschino*

And lastly, another combination. Scoop out some halved oranges. Remove the pips and pith from the flesh (and do not lose the juice), mix this with some crushed strawberries, a few stoned cherries, castor sugar and a few drops of maraschino, and refill the orange halves.

Bananas au
Rhum

*Bananas
Demerara
sugar
Lemon
Rum
Cream*

Bananas and Rum make a good combination. Try it.

Peel as many bananas as are required, and bake them, either whole or cut in half lengthwise in two or three tablespoonfuls of water, sprinkled with Demerara sugar and the juice of a lemon. After they have cooked for ten minutes, throw over them a wineglassful of rum. Serve hot or cold with whipped cream, which you can flavour, if you think fit, with lemon juice or some more rum.

JUNE

Apple and Greengage Jelly is a nice way of using a packet jelly. Cook a pound of peeled, cored and sliced apples in two ounces of sugar and a gill of water boiled together till they are tender. Whip them up with a fork till they are smooth and frothy, and then dissolve in this froth a pint packet of Chivers' greengage jelly cut into very small pieces. Pour this into a mould and let it set. When it is cold serve decorated with whipped cream.

Apple and Greengage Mould

Apples
Greengage jelly
Cream

Here is a pleasant Cream made with Oranges and Sherry.

Soak an ounce of gelatine in a little cold milk. Boil up a pint of milk, and add to it the yolks of four eggs, half an orange rind finely grated, five ounces of sugar and a quarter of a pound of macaroons. Stir till it thickens, when you must add the gelatine and half a wineglassful of sherry. Strain, cool and mix in some cream and a few glacé cherries cut in small bits. Pour into a mould and serve cold.

Orange and Sherry Cream

Gelatine
Milk
Eggs
Orange
Macaroons
Sherry
Cream
Glacé cherries

While we are on the subject of oranges, a simple Orange *Soufflé* can be quickly prepared by whipping up some whites of eggs to a stiff froth, adding castor sugar and orange juice. You could, of course, flavour such a mixture with any other fruit juice, strawberry, lemon, or with chocolate or coffee.

Orange Soufflé

Eggs
Sugar
Oranges

A light savoury, or egg course, suitable for this month can be made by beating up an egg with a gill of cream, or milk, salt, pepper and a dessertspoonful of grated cheese, a mixture of Gruyère and Parmesan being the best. Beat for a few minutes, pour into little *cocottes* and bake in a hot oven for ten minutes. Serve very quickly before the *soufflés* have time to sink. This quantity is really enough for two.

Little Cheese Soufflés

Egg
Cream
or Milk cheese

125

JUNE

Two elegant extras, which will help to make June meals more appetising, are *Grissini* and *Brioches*. The first, those long sticks of bread which we have enjoyed so much in Italian restaurants, are very easy to make, and have been known to keep the most fidgety eater quite quiet.

Grissini
Flour
Butter
Baking powder
Water
possibly Milk or
Egg

Mix half a pound of flour, half an ounce of butter, a saltspoonful of baking powder and a pinch of salt with boiling water in a basin, but see that the mixture is not too moist. Knead it out till it is quite smooth, then roll it into sticks about eight or nine inches long and about the same thickness as an ordinary lead pencil. Bake these in a fairly slow oven till they are quite hard and a golden biscuit colour. If you like you can paint a little milk over them, or some beaten egg, before baking.

Brioches
Flour
Yeast
Water
Salt
Sugar
Milk
Butter
Eggs

The second extra we have all loved at the pastry-cook's; but sometimes shops are distant, or they have no *Brioches* ready. In that case it is always simpler to have one's own supply. This is quite an easy recipe, too, but like many good things it demands a little trouble—which, of course, no *Brioche*-lover will refuse.

Sift a pound of flour. Hollow a quarter of it and put in a quarter of an ounce of fresh yeast. Mix together with enough tepid water to make a soft paste, roll it in a ball, make a right-angled slit in the top, put it in a basin, cover it and leave it in a fairly warm place, to make the leaven.

Make a hollow in the remainder of the flour, and put in a quarter of an ounce of salt, an ounce and a half of sugar melted in two tablespoonfuls of milk, four ounces of butter, and four eggs. Mix from the centre, and then knead well for a few minutes.

Hollow, add another egg, mix, knead again for two minutes, and add and mix in a final egg, six in all. Spread out the paste and lay thinly on it six ounces of butter softened to the same consistency, and work this in in small portions till it is thoroughly mixed.

Now turn the paste over and spread the leaven (which should by now be twice its original size) upon it. Mix it well, put the whole into a basin, cover it, and leave it in a temperate room for five or six hours. At the end of this time it should be turned out on to a floured board and beaten with the flat of the hand. Return it to the basin, let it ferment for another six hours, take it out, beat it again, and it is then ready to be baked in the ordinary way.

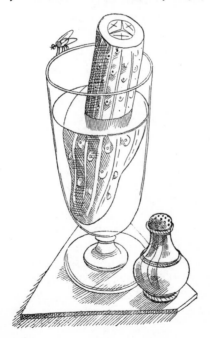

IMPORTANT POINTS TO REMEMBER

1. In many of the recipes that follow, *simmering* will be mentioned. Remember that food will simmer just as well in the lower oven as on the simmering (right-hand) hot-plate. To use the lower oven for this purpose not only gives more space on the hot-plate, but, when the hot-plate is not in use, conserves the heat of the stove.

2. It is important to see that the hot-plate lids are always kept down when not in use. Do not keep kettles boiling on the hot-plate. You will only be wasting heat. Remember that the water in the Aga tank is nearly boiling, and will boil up in a minute or two.

3. A wipe in time saves nine. Keep the Aga top clean with a damp cloth as you use it.

N.B.—The flues of the Aga Cooker should be cleaned quarterly (see page 20). Make a note to do so this month.

JULY

THE FOOD OF THE MONTH

Food which is in season all the year round is given in the table on page 44.

Note.—Newcomers are printed in italics.

FISH

Sea Fish

Hake	Herrings
Mackerel	Whitebait

River Fish

Eels	Salmon
	Trout

Shell Fish

Crabs

MEAT

Lamb

POULTRY

Ducklings   Guinea-fowl

GAME

Buck Venison

VEGETABLES

Globe Artichokes

Asparagus	Aubergines
Broad Beans	Cauliflower
Green Corn	Green Peas
New Potatoes	*Runner Beans*
Shallots	Spinach
Vegetable Marrows	

FRUIT

Apricots	Cherries
Currants	*Figs*
Gooseberries	Melons
Raspberries	Strawberries

EMPIRE IMPORTED FRESH FRUIT

Apples	Grape Fruit
Limes	Naartjes
Pears	Oranges

JULY

The following recipes are given during this month:

Cauliflower Soup

*Cauliflower
Onion
Celery
Bayleaf
Flour
Butter
White stock
Milk*

There are days even in July when soups are welcome. Cauliflower Soup may well be one of them.

Cook a cauliflower in boiling salted water for twenty minutes, then cut it in half. Set half aside and keep it warm, and pass the other through a coarse sieve. Now chop a small onion and a stick of celery (in the summer use celery salt in the seasoning) and fry them for a few minutes in two ounces of butter with a bayleaf. Take out the bayleaf and stir in an ounce of flour. Add to this two pints of white stock, stirring well. Meanwhile boil a pint of milk and mix it with the cauliflower purée and then add it to the stock. Season to taste, strain, and put in the rest of the flower which you have broken into small pieces. Serve with *croûtons* of fried toast.

Eggs en cocotte

Eggs *en cocotte* make a pleasant summer course, and are by no means unacceptable for breakfast. The little *cocottes*, like tiny earthenware saucepans, are familiar to us all. The simplest way is to butter the *cocotte*, break the egg into it, put a dot of butter on it and bake in a tin of boiling water for seven or eight minutes. Some cover them, some do not: it is a matter of taste. Eat the eggs out of the *cocotte*, or turn them out and serve on buttered toast.

Eggs en cocotte à la crème

These little dishes are susceptible of the same variations as eggs *sur le plat*. To cook them *à la crème*, you simply put into each *cocotte* a tablespoonful of boiling cream before breaking in the egg. A mixture of chopped bacon, mushrooms and onion makes a very savoury foundation for a first course at luncheon, or chopped chicken's liver, onion and bacon. To cook them plainly and pour a little hot tomato sauce over them is favoured by some, or a rich mushroom sauce could be used, and so on.

Fillets of Sole *Victoria* must find a place in your next dinner-party. Fold the fillets in two and cook them in butter and the liquor from some mushrooms. Place the fillets in a circle on a dish and place in the centre pieces of lobster and truffles which have been tossed in butter. Cover the whole with Béchamel sauce, sprinkle over the top grated Parmesan cheese, pour over a little melted butter and put in the oven till golden. Or the fillets could, of course, be stuffed with the lobster. (The truffles could be omitted in an emergency.)

Sole Victoria

Fillets of sole
Butter
Mushroom liquor
Lobster
Truffles
Béchamel sauce
Parmesan

For a Sunday supper, when tennis or the river has kept us late out of doors, this West Indian *Marinade* may be appreciated. Boil two pounds of hake, for instance, and let it get cold. Skin and bone it and put a layer in the dish in which it will be served. On this put some very thin slices of raw onion and pimentoes (which can be bought in tins if the fresh are unobtainable), a bayleaf, one or two cloves, red pepper, freshly ground black pepper and salt. Sprinkle with a few drops of olive oil here and there, and repeat these alternate layers till the supply of fish is exhausted. Finally, pour over the whole a glass of wine vinegar, and let it stand for not less than two hours.

Marinade of Fish

Boiled fish
Onion
Pimento
Bayleaf
Cloves
Red pepper
Wine vinegar
Olive oil

Devilled Crab is an excellent dish.

Flake the meat of a boiled crab and mix it with a sauce made of a quarter of a pint of white sauce, a dessertspoonful of anchovy essence, the same of chutney, a teaspoonful of chilli vinegar and the same of made mustard, seasoned with salt, pepper

Devilled Crab

Crab
Béchamel sauce
Anchovy essence
Chutney
Chilli vinegar

Mustard
Cayenne
Breadcrumbs
Parsley

and cayenne. Put the mixture back into the shell, or into little *coquilles*, cover lightly with browned breadcrumbs, and bake in a moderate oven for about a quarter of an hour. Sprinkle with chopped parsley before serving very hot.

Lobster à la Crème

Lobster
Brandy
Butter
Paprika
or Cayenne
Eggs
Cream
Sherry or
Madeira

Lobster *à la crème* would be excellent for a late supper when the host's or hostess's prowess with the chafing dish might be on view. Cut the lobster in slices (a cooked one, of course), pour a liqueur-glassful of brandy over them, and set it alight. (This preliminary might be omitted, but if you are cooking it at the table, it is a pretty start.) Then cook the pieces for a few minutes in butter, seasoning them with salt, pepper, and paprika or cayenne. While they are cooking, beat up the yolks of two eggs with a little cream, and add a dash of Sherry or Madeira. Combine this with the lobster, and stir it slowly and carefully on the lowest possible heat till the sauce is thick. It must not boil on any account.

Lobster
au gratin

Lobster
Mornay sauce
Parmesan
Cayenne or
Paprika

Lobster *au gratin* is another simple form of cooking this favourite shellfish.

The simplest way to do this is to warm up the pieces of a cooked lobster in Mornay sauce. Put them and the sauce back into the shells, sprinkle with grated Parmesan and brown. The sauce should be rather thick, and flavoured with a little cayenne or paprika pepper.

Shrimps
à la chinoise

Shrimps
Mushrooms
Water
Vinegar

An original way of cooking shrimps and peas was recently shown to me. It was called Shrimps *à la chinoise*.

Soak four and a half ounces of mushrooms (very young pink ones should be used, or those in a bottle) in water with a dash of vinegar for ten minutes, then cut them into small dice. Cut the same amount of lean bacon or ham into the same-sized dice, and brown them lightly in butter. Add half a pound of shelled peas, and cook them for half an hour, covering the pan with a soup-plate containing hot water. A spoonful or two of water may be added if the peas show signs of getting hard or dry. While this is cooking, fry half a pound of shelled shrimps in butter in a separate pan. They must not get brown or dry. In yet another pan now cook the mushrooms in butter to which a small chopped onion has been added. When they are done, add the bacon and peas and shrimps, cooking them all quickly together and shaking them for a few minutes so that their flavours are slightly blended. Season to taste and serve hot.

Bacon or Ham
Peas
Onion

Veal Cutlets can be served with Apples in this way.

Season some veal cutlets, pour some melted butter over them and grill them. When they are cooked, make a few incisions in each and cover them with a paste made of butter, chopped parsley, pepper and salt. Dish them round a purée of apples, which has been made by cooking a pound of apples in a little water with sugar and a few pieces of lemon rind and passing it through a sieve. Tomato sauce can be handed separately, if liked.

Veal Cutlets
with Apples

Veal
Butter
Parsley
Apples
Lemon
and possibly
Tomato sauce

A cold salad of Sweetbreads and Cucumber is a happy idea.

Shred some lettuces and toss them in salad dressing or light mayonnaise. Lay them on a dish and place on them some slices of thinly sliced cooked sweetbread. Spread a mayonnaise over this and garnish with sliced cucumber.

Sweetbread
and Cucumber
Salad

Lettuces
Salad dressing
or Mayonnaise
Sweetbread
Cucumber

Ham Loaves
Potatoes
Ham
Butter
Eggs
possibly
Nutmeg and
Parsley

Breakfasts or picnics are both equally well served by these little Ham Loaves. Cook and mash a pound of potatoes and mix them with a quarter of a pound of grated lean ham, an ounce of butter, two beaten eggs, salt and pepper. Grated nutmeg and chopped parsley can be added, either or both, if you care to do so. Mould the mixture into little loaves and fry them, or bake them in the oven, in the latter case gilding them with beaten egg. Serve hot for breakfast, cold for picnics. They are not too hammy in these cold-ham-and-salad days.

Stuffed
Chicken
en Cocotte

Chicken
Onions
Mushrooms
Chicken's liver
Bacon or Pickled
pork
Potatoes
Artichoke
bottoms
Stock
White wine

The advent of Globe Artichokes demands this stuffed chicken—a young one, please.

First make a stuffing by frying in butter for five minutes two or three small onions cut in slices. When they are getting brown, take them out and put in half a dozen sliced mushrooms. Cook these for a few minutes. Chop up the liver of the chicken (or two, if you can get another), and mix it with the mushrooms and onions. Stuff the chicken with this mixture (inside, not in the crop).

Cook, in a *cocotte* large enough to hold the chicken, a couple of rashers of bacon or pickled pork cut into cubes, with a piece of butter the size of an egg. When the bacon is cooked, take it out and brown the chicken in the butter, turning it on all sides. Now put back the bacon and add half a dozen potatoes cut in thin slices and some artichoke bottoms quartered. Cook all together without a lid for half an hour. Then take everything out of the *cocotte* except the gravy, pour in a small quantity good stock and white wine, and let it reduce a little. Season, put back the chicken and the other ingredients and serve as it is. No other vegetables are needed with this admirable dish. If you do not like the taste of wine, leave it out.

Chicken Maryland is a famous dish, but we are sometimes not quite sure of its composition.

Cut the chicken in pieces, season them, dip them in butter, roll in breadcrumbs and fry them in butter. They should be served with a rasher of grilled bacon between the pieces, and surrounded by small fried cakes of maize flour and fried slices of banana. A horseradish sauce enriched with cream is sometimes handed separately.

*Chicken
Maryland
Chicken
Butter
Breadcrumbs
Bacon
Maize flour
Banana
possibly
Horseradish
sauce and Cream*

The aubergine has now come into season, and I should like to make a few suggestions for making its better acquaintance. Fried slices of aubergine we have no doubt encountered, at any rate in a *Fritto Misto*, but this exotic-looking vegetable makes an extraordinarily good dish by itself, or accompanied by meat or a meaty stuffing. So here are one or two recipes, which I hope will be tried, for they deserve it.

Aubergines à l'égyptienne. Cut as many aubergines as you want in half lengthwise, and cook them gently in butter. When they are done, drain them and remove the pulp from their insides. Put the shells on the fireproof dish on which they are to be served. Now chop up the pulp, add to it a little chopped onion which you have fried in oil, and the same quantity of finely chopped lean cooked mutton as there is pulp. Fill the shells with this mixture, sprinkle with a very little oil and cook in the oven for a quarter of an hour. Just before serving the aubergines, garnish each half with a few rings of tomato lightly cooked in oil, and sprinkle chopped parsley over them.

*Aubergines
à l'égyptienne
Aubergines
Onion
Oil
Cooked Mutton
Tomato
Parsley*

Aubergines
à la provençale

Aubergines
Tomatoes
Oil
Garlic
Breadcrumbs
Tomato sauce

Aubergines à la provençale. Prepare them as above, but instead of adding onion and mutton to the pulp, add tomatoes tossed in oil and flavoured with a little garlic. Sprinkle the halves with browned breadcrumbs, brown in the oven and surround on serving with tomato sauce.

Fried
Aubergines

Fried Aubergines. Cut the aubergines into thin rounds. Season, dredge them with flour and fry in boiling oil. They must be drained and served at once, before they lose their crispness.

Aubergines
à la turque

Aubergines
Flour
Oil
Egg
Cheese
Batter or
Egg-and-
Breadcrumbs
Parsley

Aubergines *à la turque.* Cut each peeled aubergine into six slices lengthwise. Season, dredge with flour and fry these slices in oil. Then make a sandwich of two of them and put between them a firm preparation of egg yolk and finely grated cheese. Dip these sandwiches into batter, or egg-and-breadcrumb them, and fry them. Serve with fried parsley.

Fried
Cauliflower
à la polonaise

Cauliflower can be fried with great success. Boil it till it is nearly done, then take it out and dry it. Break the head into small flowerets and fry them in butter till they are golden brown. These flowerets can then, if desired, be treated *à la polonaise,* which has already been described for *petits poussins* and asparagus.

Another way is to marinate the boiled pieces for a quarter of an hour in a mixture of equal parts of water and vinegar, then to dip each piece in batter and fry in the usual way.

Fried
Cucumber

Cucumber
Lemon
Flour

Cucumber can be fried, too, in the same way as the aubergine.

Cook some inch-thick slices of peeled cucumber in boiling water slightly salted and flavoured with lemon juice, for ten minutes. Take them out, drain

and dry them, flour them, egg-and-breadcrumb *Egg-and-*
them and fry them. Grilled meat seems sometimes *Breadcrumbs*
to demand this accompaniment.

A simple stuffed-cucumber dish is this one. Split Stuffed Baked
the peeled cucumbers lengthwise, and remove the Cucumber
seeds. Now stuff them with a mixture of fine bread- *Cucumber*
crumbs, grated onions, salt and cayenne or paprika *Breadcrumbs*
pepper bound with melted butter. Bake them with *Onions*
a little good stock, with which they should occa- *Cayenne or*
sionally be basted. *Paprika*
Butter
Stock

To return for one minute to the aubergine, and
to an Eastern dish, *Moussaká*. Moussaká

Fry some aubergines cut lengthwise, and fry some
small pieces of mutton strongly seasoned. Then
arrange layers of the aubergine and mutton, moisten
the mixture with stock and cook in the oven till the
stock has disappeared. This is served with pilaff rice
and a tomato sauce.

Another version adds tomatoes, shallots and
parsley to the aubergines, omits the stock, and simply
bakes in the oven for forty minutes.

Yet another advises the use of marrow instead of
aubergine, which may be quite satisfactory, I should
think, as a *pis-aller*.

And one I tasted not so long ago in a little Smyrnese restaurant in London was just made with slices
of potatoes and minced mutton. But the flavour was
authentic. An elastic dish, *Moussaká* (with the accent
on the last syllable), and a most useful one, which
we could well adapt to our convenience.

Flageolets are those pale green little haricot beans Flageolets
which come to us fresh in boxes. They can also be
had by the pound dried, but are not nearly so good.

They can be used simply boiled, and served with a little butter, or more delicately as a purée, known as *Purée Musard*. They are often used for thickening a purée of French beans, for which they are especially suited.

Peas with Bacon
Peas
Lettuce
Pickled pork or Bacon
Onions
Butter

We have been eating Peas for some time now, so it will do us no harm to be reminded how otherwise they can be cooked. An unusual way is to cook them in very little water with a piece of butter, the heart of a lettuce cut in four, two rashers of pickled pork or green bacon cut in small pieces, and half a dozen button onions and salt and pepper. Or you can use pork fat instead of butter. Before crying, Vandal! make the experiment yourself.

New Peas Italian fashion
Lettuce
Peas
Butter
Egg
Cream
Sugar

This is an Italian way of cooking new peas.

Wash and tie up a lettuce and cook it with a quart of new peas in half a pint of salted water to which you have added a quarter of a pound of butter. As soon as the peas are done, take out the lettuce and keep it hot. Now beat up the yolk of an egg with a quarter of a pint of cream and add it, with salt, pepper and a good pinch of sugar, to the contents of the saucepan. Stir for two or three minutes, untie the lettuce, dish it and serve it with this mixture poured over it. And eat it as a separate course, please.

Strawberries au vin
Strawberries
Sugar
Red or White Wine

Now for the sweets of July! Two more strawberry suggestions, I think. First, if you are a little tired of strawberries and cream, try just sprinkling them with sugar and adding a tablespoonful of good red or white Bordeaux. Cream should *not* be taken with this.

Strawberry Cream

The second is an easy strawberry cream. Pass half

a pound of strawberries through a hair sieve, and add three ounces of castor sugar and the juice of half a lemon or orange. Melt half an ounce of gelatine in half a teacupful of milk and strain it on to the strawberry purée. Then whip half a pint of cream and fold it into it. Put into a mould and turn out when ready to serve. This should stand on ice for some time before being eaten, if it is possible.

Strawberries
Sugar
Lemon or
Orange
Gelatine
Milk
Cream

It is time to cook some cherries, those lovely black ones whose flesh is so sweet and melting. Jules Claretie, the famous French author, has given a recipe for a Cherry Pudding called *Clafoutis Limousin*. Put three tablespoonfuls of flour and a pinch of salt into a bowl and break and mix into it one by one three eggs. Add a pint and a half of milk by degrees, and three tablespoonfuls of castor sugar. Put about a pound and a half of black cherries into a fireproof dish, and pour this mixture over them. Bake it in the oven, and serve it with more sugar sprinkled over the top.

Cherry
Pudding
Flour
Eggs
Milk
Sugar
Black cherries

Another way of serving Black Cherries is to stone a pound of them and stew them in sugar and water, gently so as to keep them whole. Let them get cold and add a couple of tablespoonfuls of Kirsch or Maraschino. In as many champagne glasses as you need place a macaroon, and on this pour your cherry compote to three-quarters of the way up the glass. A covering of stiffly whipped cream on top, and some chopped pistachio nuts on that.

Cherries
Black cherries
Kirsch or
Maraschino
Macaroons
Whipped cream
Pistachio nuts

Here is a new savoury. Take some tips of boiled asparagus and toss them in butter. Lay them on a piece of buttered toast, sprinkle them very lightly with grated Parmesan cheese, and brown quickly.

Asparagus
Tips with
Cheese
Asparagus
Parmesan

Buttered toast possibly Cream or Egg

If you wanted this dish rather richer, you could bind the tips with a little cream or the yolk of an egg before putting them on the toast. It is very good.

And here are two salads.

Potato Salad

Potatoes White Wine Oil Vinegar Chervil Parsley

A slightly different taste in potato salad can be achieved by putting your cooked potatoes, thinly sliced and still lukewarm, into a salad bowl and sprinkling them with a good glass of white wine for each pound of potatoes. Season this with oil and vinegar when it is cold, and stir in carefully a little chopped chervil and parsley.

Cucumber Salad

Cucumber Vinegar

To make an orthodox cucumber salad, you should cut the peeled cucumber into thin slices, put them on a plate and sprinkle them with salt to bring out the water. After an hour drain the slices and dress them with pepper and vinegar.

Home-made Pâté de Fois Gras

Chickens' livers or Goose livers Bacon Thyme Bayleaf Brandy or Sherry Cream and possibly Truffle

This month's elegant extra is a tip for the picnic-goers and high-class tea-party givers. It is a home-made *Pâté de Foie Gras*. Do not conjure up visions of fatted geese breathing out their last on your lawn. This is a substitute, but in certain circumstances it might not be detected. You want a pound of chickens' livers or two goose livers, and a quarter of a pound of fat bacon. Cut up the latter into small pieces and fry them slowly in a frying-pan. Add the livers cut up small, a sprig of thyme and a bayleaf. Throw in a tablespoonful of brandy or sherry, cook for about ten minutes, take out the herbs and pound in a mortar. Then pass the mixture through a very fine sieve and mix it with a little cream, salt and pepper. If you can add some small pieces of truffle, do so now. Press down into little pots and, when it is quite cold, pour a little melted butter over each.

IMPORTANT POINTS TO REMEMBER

1. In many of the recipes that follow, *simmering* will be mentioned. Remember that food will simmer just as well in the lower oven as on the simmering (right-hand) hot-plate. To use the lower oven for this purpose not only gives more space on the hot-plate, but, when the hot-plate is not in use, conserves the heat of the stove.

2. It is important to see that the hot-plate lids are always kept down when not in use. Do not keep kettles boiling on the hot-plate. You will only be wasting heat. Remember that the water in the Aga tank is nearly boiling, and will boil up in a minute or two.

3. A wipe in time saves nine. Keep the Aga top clean with a damp cloth as you use it.

> **N.B.—Drain off a pint of water from the bottom tap quarterly. This will prevent sediment accumulating in the bottom of the tank. Make a note to do so this month.**

AUGUST

THE FOOD OF THE MONTH

Food which is in season all the year round is given in the table on page 44.

Note.—Newcomers are printed in italics.

FISH

Sea Fish

Haddock   Hake
Herrings   *Skate*
Whitebait

River Fish

Eels   Salmon
Trout

Shell Fish

Crabs

MEAT

Lamb

POULTRY

Ducklings   *Ducks*
Goslings   Guinea-fowl

GAME

Blackcock   Capercailzie
Grouse   Leveret
Buck Venison
Wild Duck   Woodcock

VEGETABLES

Globe Artichokes
Aubergines
Broad Beans
Cauliflower   Green Peas
New Potatoes
Runner Beans   Shallots
Vegetable Marrows
Watercress

FRUIT

Apricots   Cherries
Currants   Figs
Gooseberries
Greengages   Melons
Mulberries   *Loganberries*
Plums
Raspberries
Strawberries

EMPIRE IMPORTED FRESH FRUIT

Grape Fruit   Limes
Naartjes   Oranges

The following recipes are given during this month:

Vegetable Marrow Soup

Milk
Water
Onion
Bayleaf
Celery
Marrow
Butter
Flour
Paprika
Cream

Vegetable Marrow Soup, like Cucumber Soup, is light enough for summer eating.

Heat a quart of milk, and add to it two cupfuls of boiling water, two tablespoonfuls of minced onion, a bayleaf, quarter of a cupful of chopped celery (it will be easier to add celery salt to the flavouring later), and a good cupful of boiled marrow passed through a sieve. Make a thickening with three table-spoonfuls of butter and the same amount of flour with a little of the soup, stir this into the soup till it thickens, and season with salt, pepper and a little paprika. Cook for ten minutes together, strain and add a little cream. Or, if you serve it in separate cups, put a teaspoonful of whipped cream into each. (This is rather for decoration than anything else, for the soup tastes better if the cream is well blended into it.)

Iced Polish Soup

Beetroot
Cucumber
Egg
Parsley
Chervil

I read somewhere the other day of an iced vegetable soup from Poland which sounded appropriate for August evenings. A beetroot cut in very small pieces was cooked in salted water, and while this was being done half a cucumber cut in thin slices was sprinkled with salt so that the water was exuded. The beetroot, cucumber, cucumber water, and the water in which the beetroot had been cooked were mixed together when cold, and to this were added slices of hard-boiled egg, chopped parsley and chervil, pepper and one well-beaten egg. It must be kept well iced, and at the very last moment pieces of ice were put into the individual cups in which this soup is served. I have not tried it yet, but I certainly shall do so.

Cold Stuffed Eggs

Cold Stuffed Eggs are useful for all meals this month, and their variety is legion. I remember that in my childhood they were invariably stuffed with anchovy, but though this is very good, it is not a patch on the many fascinating stuffings which have been and still can be devised. Escoffier has a pleasant little preamble on this subject, which should make the chests of all amateur cooks swell with expectant pride. 'The preparation of cold eggs', he says, 'is not limited by classical rules; it rests with the skill and artistic imagination of the operator, and, since fancifulness and originality are always closely allied to artistic imagination, it follows that the varieties evolved may be infinite.'

Although Escoffier includes under his heading of cold eggs, cold soft-boiled and even poached eggs, the stuffed hard-boiled egg is perhaps more suited to English palates. The principle to be observed is to mix up whatever flavouring is used with the yolk, moistening it if necessary with a little cream or even milk, or some sauce. You will be able at once to think of many savoury fillings, but here are some suggestions:

Finely chopped celery with cream, salt and pepper.

Mixed herbs and finely chopped onions, varied with chopped olives, pickled walnuts, pimentoes, and so on.

Foie gras. (Eggs Mimosa are eggs stuffed thus with *foie gras*, and covered with a sauce of one-third Béchamel and two-thirds mayonnaise sprinkled over with chopped yolks.)   Eggs Mimosa

Finely chopped lean ham. A dash of Worcester sauce can be added to this if liked.

Sardines, cod's roe, flaked haddock or kipper, tunny fish, tinned salmon, or various fish pastes, such as lobster, crab, etc.

Grated cheese.

Little pieces of very crisply fried bacon with a little chopped parsley.

Mushrooms.

AUGUST

A purée of asparagus.
Tomato purée highly seasoned, perhaps with a little grated cheese added.

These little eggs can be garnished in all manner of ways. They can be embedded in a salad, or placed on pieces of cold buttered toast, or on rings of cucumber or tomato. But in whatever form they appear, they are almost always certain to be welcome.

Salmon with Tomato Sauce

Salmon
Nutmeg
Parsley
Shallots or Onions
Claret or Cider
Tomato sauce

This is an Italian dish of Salmon.

Have the salmon cut in slices about an inch thick and put them in a buttered fireproof dish. Sprinkle them with salt, pepper, a little grated nutmeg, a teaspoonful of chopped parsley and two small shallots (or onions) finely chopped. Dot with butter, and pour over a small glassful of claret or dry cider, if the latter is preferred. Bake for about a quarter of an hour, basting well. Keep the cutlets warm, and make a tomato sauce in which the liquid from the fish has been used, and pour this over the cutlets before serving.

Salmon au Citron

Salmon
Lemons
Butter
Cream or Milk

Tinned fresh or smoked salmon can be made into an attractive dish in a hurry, if you have a few lemons in the house.

Pound the salmon well with butter, salt, pepper and the juice of a lemon, using enough butter to make the cream of the consistency you like. You will need to 'work' this paste for about a quarter of an hour, adding a little cream or creamy milk if it is too thick. Serve it in the scooped-out halves of lemons on a bed of salad. It makes an attractive and refreshing fish course, which might well be remembered as a stand-by for unexpected guests.

AUGUST

Another pleasant cold dish can be made by making a purée from the flesh of a cooked smoked haddock. Pour a thick Tartare sauce over it, and garnish with slices of tomatoes and hard-boiled eggs, and some chopped tarragon, if you can get it.

Smoked
Haddock à la
Tartare
Haddock
Tartare sauce
Tomatoes
Hard-boiled eggs
Tarragon

An appetising way of having Fried Sole in the hot weather is to cut the fillets into very thin strips about three or four inches long. Either roll them in flour, or egg-and-breadcrumb them, and fry them. Serve while they are still crisp, with a sauce according to your fancy. Somehow the sole seems much lighter when treated in this amusing way.

Fried
Sole en
blanchailles

*Fillets of
sole*
*Flour or
Egg and
breadcrumbs*

A cold Crab *Soufflé* must certainly be embarked upon this month.

Boil a crab and remove all the flesh, setting aside one claw. Now mix the rest of the flesh, seasoned with salt and pepper, with a cupful of mayonnaise sauce and the same of liquid aspic jelly. Add four leaves of gelatine dissolved in a little warm water, and stir them into the mixture. Put half this mixture into a *soufflé* dish, then half the flesh from the claw you have kept back, then the rest of the mixture, and finally the rest of the claw. When cold, turn out on to a salad of lettuce and tomato.

Cold Crab
Soufflé

*Crab
Mayonnaise
Aspic jelly
Gelatine*

Lobster *à la bordelaise* is another savoury manner of treating lobsters. Cut up two lobsters into fairly large pieces, keeping the shells, and boil these pieces for twenty-five minutes in some white wine seasoned with a clove of garlic, a *bouquet* of parsley, thyme and bayleaf, salt and pepper. The saucepan should be covered and the pieces stirred now and then. Take them out, dry them in a cloth and keep them warm. Brown two sliced onions in butter, stir

Lobster à la
bordelaise

*Lobsters
White wine
Garlic
Parsley
Thyme
Bayleaf
Onions
Tomato sauce
Cayenne*

in some flour and make a thick sauce with some of the liquor in which the lobsters were boiled. Cook for ten minutes, then add two tablespoonfuls of tomato sauce and some cayenne pepper. Warm up the pieces of lobster in this sauce and fill the shells with them. They can be browned or not.

Prawn Patties

Prawns
Sherry
Lemon
Pastry
Olives
Anchovy
essence

We have rather neglected the prawn, really because this finely flavoured fish is best eaten plainly boiled, though a very great deal is to be said for curried prawns, even when they come out of a tin. Prawn patties, however, would be delightful for an alfresco meal. They are worth the little extra trouble.

Put some boiled prawns, shelled, of course, into a wineglassful of sherry and a little lemon juice, and let them lie there for a little while. Make a flaky pastry and line your patty pans with it. Into each of these put a few prawns and slices of olives, a little anchovy essence and a teaspoonful of the marinade in which the prawns have lain. Cover the patties with paste, and bake rather quickly till the pastry is nicely browned. If you cook it too slowly, the contents may become a little dry. You can, of course, serve these patties hot, but they are most excellent when eaten cold.

Lamb Cutlets en chaud-froid

Cooked lamb cutlets
Brown chaud-froid sauce
Aspic
and possibly Truffle

Cut and trim some cutlets from a neck of lamb which has been roasted, or better, braised. Dip each in a brown *chaud-froid* sauce (for which see the chapter on Sauces) when it is nearly cold, and sprinkle them with cold melted aspic. (A slice of truffle can be put on the meat part of each cutlet before the aspic is added.) Cut them out carefully when the aspic has set, and serve them round a mound of vegetable salad bound with a little mayonnaise thinned with thick cream.

AUGUST

Fricandeau is another summer dish.

Get your butcher to cut a slice from a cushion of veal not more than an inch and a half thick. It must be cut with the grain of the meat. Beat it well, and lard it finely on the cut side. Now braise it with some good stock on a bed of sliced and fried carrots and onions (in the proportion of an ounce of each to a pound of meat), a *bouquet* of parsley, thyme and bayleaf, a clove of garlic and an ounce and a half of blanched rind of bacon or pickled pork. Cool very slowly till you can prick the meat deeply without any blood exuding. It must be cooked so long that it could be cut with a spoon, and indeed some connoisseurs demand that it should never be cut with a knife on serving—which is a little precious, I think. Anyhow, when it is cooked to your liking, dish it very carefully lest it break, clear and strain the braising liquor, pour it over the *fricandeau* and let it get cold. The meat may also be glazed, if a smarter appearance is desired, but the liquor will set to a thick jelly, which can be adorned with little heaps of cold cooked vegetables, such as peas, beans, carrots and so on.

Fricandeau

Veal
Stock
Carrots
Onions
Parsley
Thyme
Bayleaf
Garlic
Rind of bacon
or Pickled pork

An unusual Ham dish hails from Canada. Boil some Patna rice and drain it well. To this add the same weight of cooked ham finely chopped, and season well with salt, black pepper and cayenne. Mix well together and serve with a salad of lettuce.

Ham and Rice

Mousselines and *mousses* are both made in the same way, the former merely being little *mousses* which are served separately to each guest, instead of his helping himself from the larger *mousse*. We will consider *Mousselines* of Chicken, though they can be

Mousselines of Chicken

Chicken
Nutmeg
Eggs
Cream

made in the same way from other meats, poultry, game, fish and shellfish.

Cut into cubes a pound of cooked chicken meat, from which you have removed the skin and the tendons. Season it with an ounce of salt, a little pepper and nutmeg, and finely pound it to a paste. When the paste is ready, add gradually the whites of two eggs, working it well the while. Now rub it through a fine sieve, put it into a basin, stir a little more with a wooden spoon, and stir in very gradually a pint of thick fresh cream. To cook the *mousselines*, put them in the oven in *dariole*-moulds and cook *au bain-marie*, or they can be poached and well drained. They can be eaten hot with various sauces and garnishes, or cold coated with aspic. Ham and lobster *mousses* occur to us at once. Here are a few variations on the chicken theme.

Poach them and coat them with a Mornay sauce. Serve them with a heap of asparagus tips or new peas tossed in butter.

Poach them and coat them with Indienne sauce. Serve rice with these.

Poach them and coat with a *suprême* sauce flavoured with paprika. Surround with a pilaff of rice in which you have mixed some chopped tomatoes cooked in butter.

Poach them and serve them either coated with *suprême* sauce and on a bed of macaroni with tomato sauce, or coated with the same sauce on a bed of spinach. In both cases sprinkle with grated Parmesan cheese and glaze quickly in the oven.

Cold
Duckling
aux
Mandarines

A cold duckling is always a pleasure, but if it is prepared *aux mandarines*, it provides a double delight. Roast it in the oven and let it cool in the

AUGUST

liquor. When cold, lay it on a bed of rice and glaze it with aspic jelly. Surround it with tangerines hollowed and filled with a *mousse* of *foie gras*, and with little heaps of chopped aspic jelly to which, in the making, have been added the juices of the duck and the tangerines.

Hazel Hen is a most delicate bird when it has been newly shot, but cold storage does not exactly improve it for roasting. This *Salmi*, which is also suitable for other game birds, offers a good way of presenting Hazel Hen at the table.

Roast the birds, but not too much: the flesh should still be pink inside. Carve them up into pieces, removing the skin and the ends of the legs which are inclined to be bitter. Keep these pieces warm and make the following sauce:

Pound up the carcases and fry them till brown in a little butter with some chopped onion and carrot, and one or two shallots. When they are ready, add a little flour, and let that brown too. Now add a quartered tomato, a glassful of red wine, and enough stock (game stock if possible) to make the sauce the right consistency, which at the end should be thick and creamy. Cook this slowly for an hour. Towards the end of that time cook in butter some small fresh mushrooms, adding the trimmings to the sauce, which you must strain when it is finished and pour over the pieces of bird. Warm the whole thing thoroughly, and serve garnished with the mushrooms.

You can add some triangular sippets of fried bread, if you like: and if you are afraid of the pieces of bird getting dry while they are keeping warm, you can add to them a little melted meat glaze and a drop or two of burnt brandy. This *salmi* can also be made from cold cooked birds, but it will not then be as good.

Roast Saddle of Leveret

Leveret
Carrots
Onions
Shallots
Garlic
Bouquet garni
Cream
Lemon juice

While the leverets are still young, a saddle cooked in the following way is supremely good. On the bottom of a dish long enough to contain it, lay the following vegetables: half a pound of minced carrots, the same of minced onions, two ounces of minced shallots, a crushed clove of garlic and a *bouquet* of thyme, parsley, bayleaf, and if possible rosemary. The saddle, which may be improved by fine larding (though, if it is very young, this is not necessary), is laid on this and set to cook. When it is nearly done, take out the vegetables and the *bouquet* and pour in a quarter of a pint of cream. Baste occasionally with this while the cooking is completed. At the last add a squeeze of lemon juice, and serve the saddle with the cream sauce strained over it.

Cucumber au paprika

Cucumber
Onion
Lemon
Breadcrumbs
Paprika
Celery salt

We have noticed one or two forms of hot cucumber. The following is rather interesting:

Cut a large peeled cucumber into small squares, a layer of which you must put in the bottom of a buttered fireproof dish. Season these pieces with grated onion and lemon juice. Cover with breadcrumbs and dabs of butter, seasoning with plenty of paprika and some celery salt. Repeat these layers till the dish is full, ending up with crumbs and butter. Cover and bake for an hour till brown. A *sauce piquante* might well accompany this curious dish.

Stuffed Pimentoes

Pimentoes
Onions

Here is a way of stuffing pimentoes, those beautiful red or green vegetables which are now adorning the more enterprising greengrocers' windows. As a matter of fact, with a little care, the tinned ones

could be stuffed very well, so long as they are well
dried, but the fresh ones are far better.

Stock
Tomato purée
Rice

This stuffing is enough for six large ones, green
or red. Cut off the tops of the pimentoes and scoop
out very carefully, so as not to break the skins, the
seeds and the pith. Chop up two onions with the
tops of the pimentoes, and cook them in butter till
soft and nicely browned. To this add salt, pepper,
a teacupful of stock and two tablespoonfuls of
tomato purée (tinned will do, if you haven't time
to make fresh). Add to this a teacupful of rice
which has been half cooked in boiling water and
well drained, and finish cooking it in the sauce. Add
a little butter, and strain the sauce, keeping aside
the liquid which comes from it. Stuff the pimentoes
with the mixture, and cook them in the oven in a
buttered fireproof dish with the liquid poured over,
for fifteen minutes. They must be kept fairly moist
by basting, so you may need to have a little extra
stock ready. You may find it advisable to fry the
pimentoes a little (but very lightly) before stuffing
them, but it is enough usually simply to bake them.

Tomatoes can also be stuffed and baked in the
same way, but they will not take quite so long.

No repertory of potato dishes would be complete
without *maître d'hôtel* potatoes. This is one way of
cooking them.

Maître d'hôtel
Potatoes

New Potatoes
Béchamel sauce
Lemon
Butter

Boil some new potatoes and cut them into slices
while hot. Then put them into a saucepan with a
little white sauce, a squeeze of lemon juice, pepper,
salt and a little butter. Stir all together and serve hot.

Another way is to boil the potatoes in their skins,
peel them, cut them into slices, shake them well in
a saucepan with a nice piece of butter, and just before

serving sprinkle in, while shaking, some finely chopped parsley.

Potato Blanquette

Potatoes White sauce with Stock Mushrooms Egg

A *Blanquette* of them is often a novelty. While the potatoes are boiling (both for this and for the previous recipe they should be as small as possible), make a white sauce with a tablespoonful of butter, the same of flour and a breakfast-cupful of stock. Also have a few mushrooms cooking in butter. When the potatoes are done, add them with the mushrooms, salt and pepper to the sauce, and just before bringing to the table, stir in the beaten yolk of an egg.

Cream of Rice

Two seasonable sweets are Cream of Rice and Rice *à l'impératrice.*

Rice puddings can be very delicious, especially if, as my experience of the softest and creamiest rice pudding I have ever tasted tells me, it had been put in the oven last thing at night and left there till morning. But many will prefer a Cream of Rice which makes a splendid border for fruits of various kinds. It is very simple to make, though it takes a little time. All you have to do is to put a couple of tablespoonfuls of Carolina rice into a pint of cold milk. Add half a dozen lumps of sugar and a vanilla pod (which can be taken out at the end, dried, and used again). Cook *very* slowly till the milk is absorbed. Let it grow cold and then mix in a little fresh cream.

Rice à l'impératrice

Rice

A really splendid refinement of this is called Rice *à l'impératrice.*

Cook the rice as for a cream and while it is cooking cut up some preserved fruits, a little angelica and mixed peel, and some glacé pineapple into very small pieces and soak them in a little Kirsch. Add them to the rice when it is ready, and stir in also a liqueur-glassful of Kirsch. Pour into a buttered mould and, when it is cold, turn it out. If you like you can add a super-refinement in the form of a layer of red-currant jelly at the bottom of the mould, or serve the cream with a red-currant syrup.

Preserved fruits Angelica Mixed peel Glacé pine-apple Kirsch

Here are one or two salads which may be useful for August meals.

Half-Mourning Salad

If some special dish has meant the opening of a bottle of truffles and there are a few over, a salad with the picturesque name of *Demi-deuil* (Half-mourning) can be made by mixing some *julienne* strips of truffles with a *julienne* of cold waxy potatoes, and seasoning with a mustard sauce to which a little cream has been added.

Truffles Potatoes Mustard sauce Cream

Another rather unusual salad is made from apples and cucumber. Season equal parts of sliced cucumbers and apples with salt, pepper and a sprinkling of lemon juice. Bind them with a little whipped cream, and serve quickly.

Apple and Cucumber Salad

Pimentoes and Cucumber also make a good salad. Cut the pimentoes, fresh or tinned, into pieces and the cucumbers into cubes, or you can mince both finely (letting the cucumbers lie in a bowl sprinkled with salt for half an hour or so to exude their moisture), drain them, mix them, and season with pepper, oil and vinegar, and add some chopped chervil at the last or, failing that, some parsley.

Pimento and Cucumber Salad

A more elaborate cucumber salad is composed of dice of lobster, cucumber, asparagus heads, and truffles, seasoned with a mayonnaise sauce coloured with a purée of lobster coral.

Cucumber, Lobster and Asparagus Salad

Beef Salad
Beef
Tomatoes
Potatoes
Parsley
Spring onions
and possibly
Gherkins
Celery
Herring fillets
or Anchovies

Tomatoes à
l'américaine
Tomatoes
Oil
Vinegar
Onion

Cold Stuffed
Tomatoes

Beef Salad is a meal in itself.

Cut some boiled or roast beef into little cubes. Mix it with some sliced tomatoes, cold boiled potatoes, chopped parsley and spring onions. You can also add chopped gherkins, celery, herring fillets or anchovies, and it is always pleasant to have one of these fishes in it. Dress it with a simple dressing of oil, vinegar, salt and pepper.

Tomatoes are served in America as follows, as a salad or an *hors d'œuvre*. Cut them in thin rounds and marinate them for twenty minutes in oil, salt, pepper and a dash of vinegar. Arrange them on a dish with rings of very finely cut raw onion.

Tomatoes can be served cold and stuffed in a variety of attractive ways. A new flavour, for instance, can be found by filling them with tunny fish mixed with tomato juice and finely chopped herbs.

These are one or two other suggestions for stuffing them—when cold, of course:

Yolks of hard-boiled eggs mixed with mayonnaise and sprinkled with chopped parsley.

Russian salad, or any mixed cooked vegetables such as beans, peas, potatoes, carrots, moistened with mayonnaise.

Tunny Fish

Tunny Fish mixed with the above. (Tunny Fish, which can be bought in tins, makes a very delightful *hors d'œuvre* when served as it is.)

Tinned salmon mixed with a little mayonnaise.

Strips of cheese, tongue, apples and celery mixed with mayonnaise.

Tomato Ice

Quite an uncommon ice can be made, by the way, from tomatoes. Make a purée of raw tomatoes and strain it through a hair sieve. Flavour it with a little salt and pepper, and freeze slightly to make an ice of it.

IMPORTANT POINTS TO REMEMBER

1. In many of the recipes that follow, *simmering* will be mentioned. Remember that food will simmer just as well in the lower oven as on the simmering (right-hand) hot-plate. To use the lower oven for this purpose not only gives more space on the hot-plate, but, when the hot-plate is not in use, conserves the heat of the stove.

2. It is important to see that the hot-plate lids are always kept down when not in use. Do not keep kettles boiling on the hot-plate. You will only be wasting heat. Remember that the water in the Aga tank is nearly boiling, and will boil up in a minute or two.

3. A wipe in time saves nine. Keep the Aga top clean with a damp cloth as you use it.

SEPTEMBER

THE FOOD OF THE MONTH

Food which is in season all the year round is given in the table on page 44.

Note.—Newcomers are printed in italics.

FISH

Sea Fish

Bloaters	*Conger Eel*
Dab	Haddock
Herrings	*Ling*
Skate	Whitebait

River Fish

Eels	Salmon
	Trout

Shell Fish

Crabs	Oysters

MEAT

Lamb	*Pork*

POULTRY

Ducks	*Geese*
Goslings	Turkeys

GAME

Blackcock
Capercailzie
Grouse   *Hares*
Leverets   *Partridges*
Ptarmigan   *Quails*
Rabbits
Buck Venison
Wild Duck   Woodcock

VEGETABLES

Globe Artichokes
Aubergine
Brussels Sprouts
Red Cabbage   Cauliflower
Green Peas
New Potatoes
Runner Beans
Shallots
Vegetable Marrows
Watercress

FRUIT

Apricots
Blackberries
Currants   *Damsons*
Figs   Gooseberries
Grapes   Greengages
Loganberries
Melons   *Nectarines*
Peaches   Pears
Plums   *Pumpkins*
Quinces   Raspberries
Strawberries

EMPIRE
IMPORTED
FRESH FRUIT

Apples	Grape Fruit
Limes	Naartjes
Oranges	Pears
	Plums

SEPTEMBER

The following recipes are given during this month:

Pumpkin
Soup

*Pumpkin
Butter
Milk
Sugar
French roll*

Pumpkin Soup is for the adventurous who have a pumpkin thrust upon them. Cut a ripe pumpkin into small pieces, boil them for seven minutes in just enough slightly salted water to cover them, and pass them through a wire sieve. Now melt a couple of ounces of butter in a saucepan, add the purée of pumpkin and leave it on a low flame for ten minutes or so. Into this stir a pint of boiling milk, a pinch of sugar, salt and pepper. Simmer gently for a few minutes, and serve. You can put a few thin slices of stale French roll in the bottom of the tureen, if you like this habit.

Eggs sur le
plat

Eggs *sur le plat* are another form of egg-cooking which rightly has many adherents in preference to the other forms.

They can be cooked either in separate little dishes or several on a dish. Just cover the bottom of the dish with melted butter, break the egg or eggs into it, put a dash of melted butter over the yolks with a sprinkle of salt, and cook in the oven till they are lightly done. About half an ounce of butter should be used for each egg.

These eggs can be varied in as many ways as the soft-boiled eggs and eggs *en cocotte*—indeed perhaps more, as there is a little more room for the garnishings.

Eggs with
Black or
Brown
Butter

Some like Eggs in brown or black butter. They can be prepared either by cooking the eggs *sur le plat* as usual, and then covering them with a little brown butter to which a few drops of vinegar have been added; or by cooking half an ounce of butter till it is almost black. Break the eggs into this, season them and cook them. Slip them on to a dish, rinse the pan with a few drops of vinegar, and pour it with the butter over the eggs.

All sorts of extras can be added to make eggs *sur le plat* a more substantial dish. For instance, little grilled sausages with tomato sauce; sliced chicken's liver cooked in butter with a little chopped onion and paprika; a purée of spinach with a Mornay sauce (Eggs *à la florentine*); a Mornay sauce alone; small tomatoes, plain or stuffed; grilled kidney; various mincemeat and so on, besides the suggestions made for eggs *en cocotte*.

Skate *au beurre noir* is really delicious. Have the skate filleted, and boil the fillets in water to which you have added a sliced onion and a little vinegar. Cook it, drain it well and serve it with sprigs of fried parsley and black butter. The latter is made by frying a handful of parsley sprigs in butter till they are crisp and brown. Continue browning the butter without burning it, and just before serving pour it into two tablespoonfuls of boiling lemon juice. You can add a dash of vinegar, if you like.

Herrings baked with rice and tomatoes is a dish that might be tried for luncheon one day.

Take some herring fillets and cut them in half crosswise. Also skin some tomatoes, and have ready some boiled and well-drained rice. Now put a layer of the fillets in a buttered fireproof dish, and over them a layer of tomato slices. Sprinkle over this salt and pepper and a little lemon juice, or vinegar if you prefer it. Cover with the rest of the fillets, on these spread the rice and, lastly, the remaining tomato slices. Dot with butter, and bake for about three-quarters of an hour in a moderate oven.

Skate au
beurre noir
Skate
Onion
Vinegar
Parsley
Butter
Lemon

Black Butter
Butter
Lemon juice
possibly
Vinegar

Herrings
with
Tomatoes

Herrings
Tomatoes
Rice
Lemon or
Vinegar

Baked Red
Mullet, I

Red Mullet
Oil
Lemon
Parsley

Red Mullet can be cooked *en papillote* or not. Have the mullets cleaned without removing the liver. Then cook them in either of these two ways.

Wipe them and make a few gashes on either side. Season them with salt and pepper, sprinkle them with a little oil and a few drops of lemon juice and lay them on a bed of a few slices of lemon and some parsley stalks. Let them marinate thus for a couple of hours, turning them every now and then. When this process is over, bake the fish carefully, basting them the while with the marinade. It will take about twenty minutes. When serving, hand separately a little half-melted *maître d'hôtel* butter.

Baked Red
Mullet, II

Red Mullet
Oil
Lemon
Parsley
Pork fat

The second way is to marinate them as before, but when you come to bake them, wrap each in a *papillote* of strong oiled paper together with a little of the marinade, a little parsley and a few tiny bits of raw pork fat, and grill them very gently. Serve them as they are, in the paper bags.

Trout
au bleu

Trout
White wine
Onion
Carrot
Bouquet garni

Trout *au bleu* is suitable for a September repast. Make a *court-bouillon* of half a pint of white wine and the same of water, an onion and a carrot cut up, a *bouquet* of parsley stalks, thyme and bayleaf, and some salt. If you wish, you can add a leek cut up, a little celery and tarragon. Simmer this for an hour, for the last twelve minutes of which you have added a dozen peppercorns. Strain, and in this boil the trout carefully. Some people prefer melted butter with this, others a *mousseline* or *hollandaise* sauce.

Mussels
(Moules
marinière)

Mussels

One last recipe for Mussels, the renowned *Moules marinière*.

Scrape and clean the mussels well. Then chop together very finely an onion, a clove of garlic and

164

some parsley, and put this with the mussels, salt, pepper, a small piece of butter and a glassful of white wine into a saucepan. Cook quickly for about a quarter of an hour, and your mussels are ready.

Onion
Garlic
Parsley
White wine

A *Fricassée* of sausages with carrots rings the changes on our sausage dishes.

Fricassée of
Sausages with
Carrots

Parboil some carrots, cut them in slices and finish cooking them in butter. Put them in a fireproof dish with some grilled sausages (the Parisian kind), a little chopped parsley, some fat from the sausages, a small pat of butter, a few small onions chopped and fried, a drop or two of lemon juice and a glassful of dry white wine. Cook all together for a few minutes longer and serve in the same dish.

Carrots
Sausages
Parsley
Onions
Lemon
White wine

A Dutch Omelette, which is more like a pancake, is a fairly substantial dish.

Dutch
Omelette

Have ready some batter made of milk, flour, the yolks of four eggs and the whites well whisked and folded in. Make a fairly thick and fairly light pancake and slip it from the pan on to the dish on which it is to be served. Keep it warm and sprinkle on it plenty of grated Parmesan cheese. Then make another pancake, lay it on top of the first and sprinkle it with finely chopped ham. One more pancake on top of this, and then adorn the whole edifice with green peas or asparagus tips, fresh or tinned according to the season. Finally, pour a creamy white sauce over the whole, and serve very hot.

Flour
Milk
Eggs
Parmesan
Peas
or Asparagus
tips
Béchamel sauce
Ham

An unusual way of cooking liver is the following.

Liver with
Olives and
Apples

Chop up an onion and fry it in butter till brown. Stone and chop a few olives, and fry them with the bacon, and some salt and pepper, for a few minutes

Onion

Olives
Bacon
Liver
Apples

longer. Meanwhile in another pan, fry in butter or bacon fat some pieces of liver which have been rolled in flour and seasoning. Dish the pieces of liver, sprinkle the onion and olives over them, and surround them with some well-drained quarters of cored and peeled apples which have been poached in water till tender.

Chicken
en cocotte

A chicken cooked *en cocotte* is sometimes welcome as a relief from roast or boiled fowl.

Chicken
Pickled pork
Onions
Potato
Veal gravy

Brown the chicken in butter in a covered *cocotte*, till it is half cooked. Then add some small dice of pickled pork which are well fried, a dozen button onions partly cooked in butter, and twice the number of pieces of potato the size and shape of olives. Finish cooking all together. A little veal gravy can be added at the last, if you have any.

Russian
Blanquette
of Chicken

Chicken
Béchamel sauce
Cucumber
Cream

A Russian *Blanquette* of Chicken can be made from a roast fowl, as follows. Cut as many slices as are wanted from the breast of a roasted fowl (or other pieces of the fowl would do) and remove the skin. Make a Béchamel sauce, and when cooked cut up a small cucumber into thinnish slices. Stew these in the sauce and, when they are done, pour it all over the chicken, adding a few tablespoonfuls of cream at the last moment.

Partridge
à la crème

Partridge
Butter
Onion
Cream
Lemon

There will never be an end to the discussion as to which is the best of the game birds. I plump for grouse, but partridge runs him very close, and now is the time to see. Never better, I believe, than roasted, but to serve him with cream is a fetish of some. Cook him in butter in an earthenware sauce-pan with a smallish onion cut in quarters. When he is three-quarters cooked pour over him a cupful of cream into which you have mixed a few drops of lemon juice. Baste him with the cream while the cooking finishes and serve up in the saucepan.

We have been eating our grouse for some time now, but before the winter comes we should have a Grouse Salad. To make the sauce for this mix two finely minced shallots with half a dozen teaspoon-fuls of tarragon and chervil mixed together, five dessertspoonfuls of castor sugar, the yolks of two eggs, five saltspoonfuls of salt and pepper mixed, and a pinch of cayenne. Stir these ingredients into a dozen tablespoonfuls of salad oil and six dessert-spoonfuls of chilli vinegar, and finally a quarter of a pint of whipped cream. Pour this sauce over the pieces of cold grouse, which you have surrounded with beetroot and pieces of hard-boiled egg and anchovy.

Grouse Salad

Grouse
Shallots
Tarragon
Chervil
Sugar
Eggs
Cayenne
Oil
Chilli Vinegar
Cream
Beetroot
Anchovy
Hard-boiled egg

The simplest and one of the most pleasant ways of cooking a rabbit—a young one is best—is to cut him up into pieces and to put them with a good piece of butter in a casserole. Fry them till golden brown, add a few button onions, salt and pepper, put the lid on, and cook gently till the rabbit is done. Take off the cover now and then and let the water which has formed inside run into the casserole, to help with the gravy. A few mushrooms tossed in butter might be added with advantage towards the end of the cooking.

Rabbit
en casserole

Rabbit
Onions
Mushrooms

And mushrooms remind me that they are very good when cooked *à la crème*. Peel the mushrooms and remove their stalks, and if they are at all large cut them into quarters. Melt a couple of ounces of butter in a stewpan, and add the mushrooms and a

Mushrooms
à la crème

Mushrooms
Butter
Parsley

Thyme
Bayleaf
Eggs
Cream
Nutmeg

bouquet of parsley, thyme and bayleaf. Toss them on a good flame till the mushrooms are done, then take out the *bouquet* and pour off all but a very little butter. Beat up the yolks of two eggs with a gill of cream, add them to the mushrooms and stir until the mixture is cooked. Season with a little salt, pepper and grated nutmeg, and serve very hot.

Potato
Soufflé

Potato purée
Cream
Eggs

Potato *Soufflé* is a very different thing from Potatoes *soufflées*.

For the first you want about a pint of potato purée enriched with a little cream, well-whipped and fairly stiff. To this add the yolks of three eggs and their whites stiffly whisked. Season it well and cook in a buttered *soufflé* dish for about a quarter of an hour in a moderate oven.

Potatoes
soufflées

Potatoes
Frying fat

Two things must be observed about Potatoes *soufflées*. They must be very carefully cooked (for they are difficult to do), and they must be served immediately.

Peel the potatoes and cut them into slices about the thickness of a penny. Wash the pieces and dry them well and fry them in fat which must be hot, but not boiling. When they come to the top, take them out and bring the fat to the boil. Then put the pieces back, about half a dozen at a time (not more, or the temperature of the fat will be reduced), stir the fat and the potatoes should puff up. Only experience can teach you how to accomplish this dish, the success of which is better assured if you use soapy potatoes rather than floury ones.

Hot Red
Cabbage

Red cabbage

If we cannot have broad beans with our pork, we can certainly have Red Cabbage. I doubt if pickled red cabbage should even be permitted with Lancashire Hot Pot, though it is the Northern custom, and it is possible that those who abhor this unpleasant pickle have never tasted the cabbage treated in any other manner. This recipe may be a revelation to many, especially with boiled knuckle of pork. Slice a red cabbage very finely, and soak it in water for about half an hour; then put the pieces in a saucepan with an ounce of butter, a tablespoonful of chopped onion, a saltspoonful of salt, cayenne pepper and grated nutmeg. Cook with the lid on till the cabbage is tender (about an hour), then add a dessertspoonful of sugar and a tablespoonful of vinegar. Cook all together for another five minutes.

Onion
Cayenne
Nutmeg
Butter
Sugar
Vinegar

While pumpkins are in, we should try our hand at a Pumpkin Pie. Here are two ways of making it.

Pare and halve a ripe pumpkin, take out the seeds and cut it into thick slices. Stew it gently with a little water till it is tender, then pass it through a fine sieve to make a purée. Take half a pint of this, add two ounces of sugar, the yolks of two eggs, three-quarters of a pint of milk, a little mace or nutmeg, and at the last the two egg whites stiffly frothed. Put this mixture into a pie-dish, cover with short-crust paste, as for an ordinary pie, and bake in a quick oven.

Pumpkin Pie,
I

Pumpkin
Eggs
Milk
Nutmeg
Pastry

This is a simpler method. Pare, halve and cut the pumpkin into thin slices, removing the seeds. Put the slices into a pie-dish, seasoning each layer with sugar and a little allspice. Cover with paste and bake as before.

These pies can both be served hot or cold.

Pumpkin Pie,
II

Pumpkin
Allspice
Pastry

Pears or
Peaches à la
Condé

*Pears or Peaches
Vanilla pod
Rice
Apricot
syrup
Kirsch*

Pears or
Peaches
à la Cardinal
*Pears or Peaches
Vanilla pod
Raspberry purée
Kirsch
Almonds*

Egg and
Cheese
Toast
*Hard-boiled eggs
Cheese
Mustard*

Macaroni
Cheese
(Swiss
fashion)
*Macaroni
Cheese
Breadcrumbs*

Endive and
Orange Salad

*Endives
Oranges
Mustard
Cream
Cayenne*

Pears and peaches can each be used in the following ways, *à la Condé* and *à la Cardinal.*

For the first, poach the pears or peaches in sugared water to which you have added a vanilla pod, let them get cold and dish them on a border of cream of rice, covering them with apricot syrup flavoured with Kirsch.

For the second, poach the fruit as before, dish them when they are cold, and cover them with a very sweet raspberry purée flavoured with Kirsch and sprinkled with splintered fresh almonds.

Egg and Cheese Toast is a new savoury to many.

Rub the yolks of two hard-boiled eggs through a sieve, mix them with an ounce of butter and two ounces of grated cheese, and add salt and pepper and a little made mustard. Spread this mixture on squares of buttered toast pretty thickly, and brown them in a sharp oven.

The Swiss manner of making a Macaroni Cheese is preferred by many.

Cook the macaroni in salted boiling water for ten minutes, then drain it. Now in a buttered fireproof dish put a layer of macaroni, sprinkle it well with grated cheese, and so on, ending with cheese. Cover this with breadcrumbs, dot with butter and cook in the oven till golden.

And here are four more salads.

Endive and Orange combine very well. Wash some endives (the long white kind), removing all the discoloured leaves, and cut them in half lengthwise. Peel an orange or two and cut the rind into very thin strips. Boil these in water for a few minutes, and let them get cold. Arrange the endives in a dish and pour over them a sauce made of mustard, cream, salt, pepper and a little cayenne— the proportions to your taste's discretion. Sprinkle the orange strips over all.

A Spanish salad can be made as follows. Peel and quarter some small tomatoes and cut some pimentoes (tinned ones are perhaps best for this) into very thin strips. Mix these with plainly cooked rice which has been allowed to grow cold, and add a little crushed garlic, and onion and parsley finely chopped. Season with oil and vinegar.

Spanish Salad
Tomatoes
Pimentoes
Rice
Garlic
Onion
Parsley
Oil
Vinegar

An Alsatian Salad affords a good way of using up various 'scraps'. Cut some cold boiled waxy potatoes into small pieces, and mix them with any or all of the following (with any additions or omissions you feel like): chopped cold chicken, small pieces of cooked beef, ham or bacon, anchovies or herrings in oil cut up small, beetroot, gherkins, and so on. Season with oil, vinegar, salt and pepper. This should be done about an hour before serving, so that the salad absorbs some of the dressing. Mix again at the last and sprinkle with chopped parsley and onion, if you like it.

Alsatian Salad
Potatoes
Chicken
Beef
Ham or Bacon
Anchovies or Herrings
Beetroot
Gherkins
Oil
Vinegar
Parsley
Onion

Peaches and Plums can easily be pickled at home, and provide a very delightful adjunct to our dishes of cold meat. And Empire fruit is cheap enough to help us here.

Dip the peaches in boiling water for a moment, and then rub their skins off. Halve them and take out the stones, and stick two cloves into each half. Make a syrup of two pounds of brown sugar, an ounce stick of cinnamon and a pint of vinegar by boiling for twenty minutes, and cook the peaches

Pickled Peaches

Peaches
Cloves
Brown sugar
Cinnamon
Vinegar

Pickled Plums

Plums

Brown sugar
Cinnamon
Vinegar

in it, a few at a time, till they are soft. Let them get cold, and bottle them.

Plums can be pickled in the same way, halving and stoning them, but omit the cloves.

IMPORTANT POINTS TO REMEMBER

1. In many of the recipes that follow, *simmering* will be mentioned. Remember that food will simmer just as well in the lower oven as on the simmering (right-hand) hot-plate. To use the lower oven for this purpose not only gives more space on the hot-plate, but, when the hot-plate is not in use, conserves the heat of the stove.

2. It is important to see that the hot-plate lids are always kept down when not in use. Do not keep kettles boiling on the hot-plate. You will only be wasting heat. Remember that the water in the Aga tank is nearly boiling, and will boil up in a minute or two.

3. A wipe in time saves nine. Keep the Aga top clean with a damp cloth as you use it.

N.B.—The flues of the Aga Cooker should be cleaned quarterly (see page 20). Make a note to do so this month.

173

OCTOBER

THE FOOD OF THE MONTH

Food which is in season all the year round is given in the table on page 44.

Note.—Newcomers are printed in italics.

FISH

Sea Fish

Bloaters	Conger Eel
Dabs	*Gurnet*
Haddock	Herrings
Ling	Skate

Smelts

River Fish

Eels

Shell Fish

Crabs	Oysters

MEAT

Pork

POULTRY

Ducks	Geese
Goslings	Turkeys

GAME

Blackcock
Capercailzie

Grouse	Hares
Leverets	Partridges
Pheasants	*Plovers*
Ptarmigan	Quails
Rabbits	*Snipe*

Teal
Doe Venison

Widgeon	Wild Duck

Woodcock

VEGETABLES

Globe Artichokes	
Aubergines	*Broccoli*
Brussels Sprouts	
Red Cabbage	Cauliflower
Celeriac	*Horseradish*
Parsnips	
Runner Beans	
Shallots	
Spanish Onions	
Watercress	

FRUIT

Apricots
Blackberries

Damsons	Grapes
Medlars	Melons
Nectarines	Peaches
Pears	Plums
Pumpkins	Quinces

EMPIRE IMPORTED FRESH FRUIT

Apples	Grape Fruit
Limes	Oranges
Naartjes	Peaches
Pears	Plums

The following recipes are given during this month:

OCTOBER RECIPES

Minestrone

White stock
Any uncooked vegetables
Parsley
Bacon
Macaroni or Spaghetti
Cheese

The season of soups is upon us. Let us venture upon a few new ones. *Minestrone,* for instance, so beloved of Italians, and indeed of nearly all who have once tasted this national masterpiece. For this soup you will want some veal or chicken stock, and in it you must boil any vegetables that are at hand: potatoes, carrots, turnips, all cut in small slices, some shredded cabbage, a few onions sliced and lightly fried, chopped parsley, little pieces of lean bacon, a clove of garlic if you like it (but this should not remain in the soup for more than a quarter of an hour). Do not stint the vegetables, as there should be plenty, and introduce them into the stock in the order of their cooking—that is to say, put in first those that take the longest time to cook, so that all are finished together. About twenty minutes before serving, throw in some inch-long pieces of macaroni or spaghetti. Grated cheese sprinkled on each helping at the table is a *sine qua non.*

Creole Rabbit Soup

Rabbits
Water
Onion
Mace
Bayleaf
Cayenne
Rice
Sherry

A Creole Soup made from Rabbit shall be our next experiment.

Cut two young rabbits into small pieces and put them in a stewpan with two quarts of cold water. Chop up an onion and add it to the water, with a blade of mace and a bayleaf. Bring to the boil and simmer for two hours. Now add salt, pepper and cayenne pepper, and half a cupful of rice. Simmer for another hour, and when serving add a couple of tablespoonfuls of sherry.

The weather will now allow us to eat our stuffed eggs hot, an unfamiliar way, perhaps. Ingenuity can again be exercised in the composition of the stuffings and in the choice of sauce to accompany it. Here are one or two variations.

Having halved the eggs, chop up the yolks with an onion, a few fillets of anchovy, a little parsley and some pepper. Cook this in butter for a few minutes, then stuff the whites with it, put them in a fireproof dish, sprinkle with breadcrumbs, a dab of butter on each and brown under the grill or in the oven. You could serve a tomato sauce with this if you cared to.

Hot Stuffed Eggs, I
Hard-boiled eggs

Onion
Anchovy
Parsley
Breadcrumbs
possibly
Tomato sauce

Cook a few mushrooms in butter for about ten minutes. Season them with salt, pepper and a squeeze of lemon juice and chop them up with the egg yolks, binding with a little Béchamel sauce. Stuff the eggs with this, put them in a fireproof dish with some of the sauce poured round them, and brown slowly in the oven.

Hot Stuffed Eggs, II

Hard-boiled eggs
Mushrooms
Lemon
Béchamel sauce

Plaice can be cooked with Mushrooms too.
Scald the fish, make scores in the top and rub into them a tablespoonful of butter with a little salt and pepper. Let it bake in the oven in a buttered fireproof dish for a quarter of an hour, and meanwhile make a sauce of butter, flour and fish stock. Add to this sauce a few mushrooms, a sprig of thyme and basil (or a very little of these herbs dried), two sprays of parsley and six allspice all chopped very finely. Cook for five minutes longer, pour it over the fish, return the dish to the oven and cook for another quarter of an hour.

Plaice cooked with Mushrooms

Plaice
White sauce
Mushrooms
Thyme
Basil
Parsley
Allspice

Smelts are once more in season. Fried smelts are the best, I think, but much can be said for them when they are baked like this:
Arrange them in a dish (in which you will serve

Baked Smelts

Smelts
Anchovy
essence

Lemon
White wine
Cayenne
Ground mace
Breadcrumbs

them) in which you have put a little butter, a drop or two of anchovy essence, the juice of a lemon and a glass of white wine. Sprinkle them with salt, cayenne pepper and a little ground mace, cover them with breadcrumbs, dot them with butter and bake till they are brown.

Baked Stuffed
Smelts

By the dainty-fingered, smelts can be stuffed with chopped fried onions, mushrooms, oysters and parsley bound together with a thick white sauce. But not for me.

Sole
Lyonnaise

Fillets of sole
Carrot
Celery
Parsley
Clove
Thyme
Bayleaf
Water
Onion

Here is a good way of cooking Sole.

Have a sole filleted, and put the trimmings into a saucepan with a small carrot sliced, half a stick of celery also sliced, a teaspoonful of parsley, a clove, a *bouquet* of parsley, thyme and bayleaf, and enough water to cover them. Bring to the boil, simmer for an hour and strain. Fry a sliced onion in butter till golden, add half an ounce of flour and stir in half a pint of the fish liquor till it thickens. Leave this on the side of the fire, having seasoned it, and cook the sole by tying the fillets into knots, putting them into a buttered fireproof dish with a little butter, covering them with buttered paper and baking them in the oven for a quarter of an hour. When they are done, add their liquor and a dessertspoonful of chopped parsley to the sauce, which you will pour over the fillets.

South
African Meat
Custard

Bread
Milk
Onions

South African dishes do not, I find, differ very much from what we are used to at home; but this one does a little.

Soak a thick slice of bread in half a pint of milk, and mash well with a fork so that there are no lumps. Now fry two medium-sized onions, sliced, in an ounce of butter, and when they are cooked add to them the baked bread, two tablespoonfuls of curry powder, a dessertspoonful of sugar, half a dozen almonds finely chopped, a tablespoonful of lemon juice, an egg, half a teaspoonful of salt and two pounds of lean beef finely chopped. Mix all this well together, and put into a buttered pie-dish. Beat up another egg with the milk left from soaking the bread (it must be made up to a good quarter of a pint), season with salt and pepper, and pour over the mixture in the pie-dish. Bake till the custard is set. Cooked or uncooked beef can be used, but the latter will take about twice as long to cook.

Curry powder
Sugar
Almonds
Lemon
Egg
Beef

This is the Provençal way of cooking a leg of lamb or mutton, and very well worth trying. Lard a leg of lamb or mutton with about a dozen inch-long fillets of anchovy, and put a little piece of garlic near the bone. Roast it in the usual way, basting it well. Keep it hot and clear the gravy of grease.

Roast Leg of Mutton à la provençale

Mutton
Anchovy
Garlic

The leg should be served with the following sauce. Cook two small onions and two shallots, both finely chopped, in a little butter; sprinkle in a little flour and cook a short while longer. Chop up two anchovy fillets and two or three gherkins, and add these with a small spoonful of tomato purée and the gravy from the meat to the onions and flour. Stir well, cook a little longer, season well and serve with the joint.

For the Sauce

Onions
Shallots
Anchovy
Gherkins
Tomato purée

Frikadeller are a kind of meat rissole, made either of veal or, in the Danish fashion, of pork. They can be made of raw or cooked meat. (These quantities are for ten of them.)

With raw meat. Mix a pound of very finely chopped meat with two-thirds of a pound of butter.

Frikadeller, I

Raw Veal or Pork
Butter
Breadcrumbs
Eggs

179

Nutmeg
Onion
Stock

Add five ounces of well-pressed breadcrumbs soaked in stock, two beaten eggs, half an ounce of salt, a little pepper and grated nutmeg, and two ounces of chopped onion cooked in butter without browning. Mix well together, divide into ten portions, which you can roll into balls or shape into round flat cakes, brown them on both sides in butter and finish cooking them in the oven.

Frikadeller, II

Cooked veal
Nutmeg
Potatoes
Onion
Egg
Parsley

With cooked meat. Put into a bowl large pinches of salt and pepper, and a little grated nutmeg. Add the contents of three medium-sized baked potatoes, three ounces of chopped onion fried in butter without browning, a pound of finely chopped cooked veal (using the fat and lean), one egg and a tablespoonful of chopped parsley. Mix, divide and cook as in the recipe already given.

These *frikadeller* can be served with a purée of vegetables, and with a *sauce piquante*. In Denmark they are accompanied by a brown or tomato sauce, and sometimes even with beetroot or cucumber or some pickled peaches.

Casserole of
Tripe

Tripe
Oil
Vinegar
Shallot or
Onion
Mushrooms
Flour
Tomato purée
Breadcrumbs

A Casserole of Tripe is an inexpensive and excellent dish.

Cut some well-cooked tripe into strips and marinate it for a little in oil and vinegar in equal parts. While it is soaking, fry a minced shallot, or onion, golden in butter, and add half a pound of mushrooms cut in thin slices. Cook for ten minutes or so, then remove them. Stir into the butter an ounce of flour, add two cupfuls of fresh tomato purée and stir till the sauce thickens. Butter a casserole, and put into it a layer of half the tripe, then a third of the sauce, all the mushrooms, more sauce and half a cupful of breadcrumbs. On this spread the remainder of the tripe, then the rest of the sauce and more breadcrumbs. Dot with butter, and bake in the oven for about twenty minutes, when the top should be an elegant brown.

Veal makes an uncommon pudding.

Veal Pudding
Veal
Ham, Bacon or Pickled Pork
Suet paste

Cut two pounds of lean veal into smallish pieces, keeping the bones and trimmings aside. Also cut up half a pound of ham, bacon or pickled pork into thin strips. Line a basin with suet paste, put in the meat, with here and there the pieces of bacon, seasoning well with salt and pepper, and proceed as when cooking a beefsteak-and-kidney pudding.

Another American dish of chicken is made in this way.

Chicken Croquettes with Oysters
Cooked Chicken
White sauce
Celery salt
Cayenne
Lemon
Onion
Oysters
Egg and Breadcrumbs

Moisten a cupful of cold finely chopped chicken with a little white sauce, seasoning it with salt, celery salt, cayenne pepper, lemon juice and onion juice. Parboil as many large oysters as you will need, drain them and cover them with the chicken mixture. Roll these little croquettes in breadcrumbs, then in egg, and then in more breadcrumbs, and fry in deep fat.

The sauce for this dish should be made with butter and flour and some of the liquor in which the oysters were cooked, and enriched with cream.

Partridges with Cabbage is a remarkable way of using old birds. Allow half a partridge to each person.

Partridges with Cabbage
Cabbage
Partridges
Carrot
Onion
Bacon
Stock
Parsley

Cut a good-sized savoy into four, and boil it. While it is cooking put the partridges into a casserole with some butter, a carrot, an onion, a piece of fat bacon, salt and pepper, and brown on a moderate fire. Then add a tablespoonful of flour,

Thyme
Bayleaf
Sausages

mix in and pour on a cupful of stock. Also put in a *bouquet* of parsley, thyme and bayleaf. Cover and boil for twenty minutes. After this is done put in the cabbage and a few chipolata sausages. They must all be just covered with the sauce. Add a little more stock if necessary. Cover the casserole again and cook very gently till the birds are done, which will be a good hour at least. Then put the cabbage on a dish and place on top the partridges, untrussed and halved, and the sausages.

Pheasant
à la crème

Normandy
Pheasant

Pheasant
Butter
Apples
Cream

Pheasant can be worthily cooked *à la crème* in the same manner as partridge, which I described last month. To cook him in the Normandy fashion will appeal to many. Fry him well in butter till he is nicely browned, and meanwhile toss in butter half a dozen peeled, cored and finely chopped apples. Put the pheasant in a casserole on a layer of apple, putting the rest round him, and sprinkle over the bird three or four tablespoonfuls of cream. Cover the casserole and cook in the oven for about half an hour. Serve in the same dish.

Brussels
Sprouts
au gratin

Brussels sprouts
Butter
Nutmeg
Cheese
possibly
Cream

Brussels sprouts can often be made more attractive if, after they have been cooked, they are put back into the pan with a good piece of butter, some pepper and a little grated nutmeg; then put into a fireproof dish, sprinkled with some grated cheese, perhaps moistened with a little cream, which is browned quickly.

Stuffed
Spanish
Onions

Onion

Spanish onions lend themselves to a variety of stuffings, for instance the following: Fry lightly a teaspoonful of minced onion in a tablespoonful of oil and butter mixed. Add to this four tablespoonfuls of chopped mushrooms (the washed parings and stalks will be even better than the heads), and stir it over the flame till the moisture from the mushrooms has disappeared. Then season with salt, pepper, grated nutmeg and a coffeespoonful of finely chopped parsley. Parboil the onions, scoop out the insides, and chop up the flesh you have taken out with an equal quantity of the mixture just described. Finish their cooking by braising. You can elaborate this by adding some sausagemeat to the stuffing mixture, and serve with a tomato or brown sauce. You can also stuff them with spinach, with a risotto, with potato combined with their flesh, or with semolina cooked in stock and flavoured with grated Parmesan cheese. Turnips can also be presented stuffed with this last mixture.

Butter
Oil
Mushrooms
Nutmeg
Parsley
and perhaps
Sausagemeat

Stuffed
Turnips

Tinned pimentoes can be combined with potatoes in this manner. Peel some potatoes and scoop them out into little balls with a special scoop till you have a quart of balls. Throw them into cold water as you scoop them out, and, when they are all done, drain them well and fry till tender in deep fat. Fry two thin slices of Spanish onion in butter till golden, take them out, and in the same fat fry lightly two large tinned pimentoes cut in small pieces. Add the fried potatoes, mix together, sprinkle with a tablespoonful of chopped parsley, and serve very hot.

O'Brien
Potatoes

Potatoes
Tinned
pimentoes
Spanish onion
Parsley

Boil a dozen or so small waxy potatoes. To devil them, put two good tablespoonfuls of butter which have been combined with a teaspoonful of made mustard into a deep frying-pan, add a tablespoonful of vinegar, a little salt and a pinch of cayenne. Cook this mixture for three or four minutes, shaking the pan well; put in the warm potatoes, add the yolks of two eggs well beaten up and serve practically at once.

Devilled
Potatoes

Potatoes
Butter
Mustard
Vinegar
Cayenne
Eggs

Potato Cake

Potatoes
Bacon or
Onion

Everyone knows the old way of cooking up cold mashed potatoes by frying a cake of them in the frying-pan under a plate. But many forget that this dish is far nicer if it is made with freshly boiled and mashed potatoes, which can be mixed with tiny pieces of crisply fried rashers of bacon or with roughly chopped onion fried separately in butter till golden.

Apples à la Normande

Apples
Butter
Breadcrumbs
Calvados or
Brandy or
Maraschino
Red-currant
jelly

This way of baking apples comes from Normandy. Core some apples, but do not peel them, and fill up their centres with fresh butter. Sprinkle a fireproof dish with brown breadcrumbs (after buttering it, of course), put the apples on this and bake them in the oven, adding more butter from time to time as it is absorbed by the apples. When they are quite done, pour half a teaspoonful of Calvados (if you can get it, for this is the authentic flavouring), or brandy or Maraschino in each centre, powder with sugar and put on top a spoonful of some red jam or jelly, red-currant jelly being the best.

Pears Bonne Femme

Pears
Cinnamon
Red wine

Two ways of baking pears.
One. Wash, but do not peel, some cooking pears, then cook them in the oven in some water with a little sugar and cinnamon. They should cook very slowly indeed. Half-way through their cooking, add a glass of red wine, which should have practically disappeared by the time the pears are ready. Dish them and pour over them what syrup there is left.

Pears au beurre

Pears
Butter
Sugar

Two. Peel some pears and cut them into thin slices. Put these into a fireproof dish, adding sugar and little pieces of butter between each layer. Brown in the oven.

OCTOBER

Apples can be cooked in the same way, they tell me.

Apples
au beurre

Apples make good puddings, and can even make tapioca palatable. Here is the way, for whoever cares to try it. Boil three tablespoonfuls of large tapioca very slowly in a pint of milk flavoured with lemon peel for three or four hours, and while this is finishing stew in syrup half a dozen apples, peeled, cored and cut in not-too-small pieces. Put half the tapioca in the fireproof dish and on it half the apples. Repeat this, spread plenty of apricot jam over the top, and bake in the oven for twenty minutes. Serve hot, of course, and I have an idea that marmalade might advantageously be substituted for the jam.

*Apples and
Tapioca*

*Apples
Tapioca
Milk
Lemon
Apricot jam
or Marmalade*

We may be lucky and get some early celery at the end of the month. It mixes well with cheese, whether hot or cold. This is the hot one.

Cook some inch-long pieces of celery in slightly salted boiling water. Drain it and stir with a tablespoonful of butter for a minute or so. To this add a cupful of white sauce made with a little milk and some of the water in which the celery was boiled. Season well, add some grated cheese and a teaspoonful of lemon juice. Pour into a dish, sprinkle with more cheese and brown.

Celery and
Cheese, I

*Celery
White sauce
Cheese
Lemon*

Although we often eat celery with our cheese, this dish may nevertheless surprise our friends. Have some Gorgonzola or Stilton cheese mixed with an equal quantity of butter, and having opened the hearts of two or three good heads of celery, stuff the hollow part of each stick with the mixture. Having done this, press the sticks back so that they

Celery and
Cheese, II

*Celery
Gorgonzola or
Stilton cheese
Butter*

185

will resume their natural shape and serve the heads, in all innocence, on a large flat dish, cutting the pieces across when you want to help them. A few kinds of dry biscuits, and you have a climax to your meal the flavour of which will be appreciated—and your ingenuity commended.

Celery and
Cucumber
Salad

Celery
Cucumber
Mayonnaise
Radishes
Hard-boiled egg
Gherkins
Parsley

Celery makes a good salad with cucumber.

Shred the white part of a head of celery into fine strips, leave it in water for about half an hour, then drain and dry it. Peel the cucumber, cut it into one-and-a-half-inch lengths, and shred it in the same way as the celery. Now mix these together with some salt and pepper and a thinnish mayonnaise sauce, heap the salad in a dish, garnish it with radishes and hard-boiled egg, and sprinkle over it a teaspoonful of finely chopped gherkins and parsley mixed together.

Gnocchi alla
Romana

Semolina
Milk
Egg
Butter
Cheese
Nutmeg

Cheese dishes are always welcome for luncheon. *Gnocchi alla Romana* are a savoury form of semolina. Sprinkle a third of a pound of semolina into a pint of boiling milk, and after adding salt, pepper and grated nutmeg, simmer gently for twenty minutes. Now, off the fire stir in the yolk of an egg, and spread out the mixture to cool in a layer about half an inch thick. When cold, cut it into small rounds or squares, put these pieces in a buttered fireproof dish, sprinkle them liberally with a mixture of grated Gruyère and Parmesan cheese and a little melted butter, and bake in a moderate oven for twenty minutes. Some people like to add a thick tomato sauce to this exquisite dish.

1. In many of the recipes that follow, *simmering* will be mentioned. Remember that food will simmer just as well in the lower oven as on the simmering (right-hand) hot-plate. To use the lower oven for this purpose not only gives more space on the hot-plate, but, when the hot-plate is not in use, conserves the heat of the stove.

2. It is important to see that the hot-plate lids are always kept down when not in use. Do not keep kettles boiling on the hot-plate. You will only be wasting heat. Remember that the water in the Aga tank is nearly boiling, and will boil up in a minute or two.

3. A wipe in time saves nine. Keep the Aga top clean with a damp cloth as you use it.

N.B.—Drain off a pint of water from the bottom tap quarterly. This will prevent sediment accumulating in the bottom of the tank. Make a note to do so this month.

187

NOVEMBER

THE FOOD OF THE MONTH

Food which is in season all the year round is given in the table on page 44.

Note.—Newcomers are printed in italics.

FISH

Sea Fish

Bloaters	*Cod*
Conger Eel	Dabs
Gurnet	Haddock
Herrings	Ling
Skate	Smelts

Sprats

River Fish

Eels

Shell Fish

Oysters

MEAT

Pork

POULTRY

Ducks	Geese
Turkeys	

GAME

Blackcock
Capercailzie

Grouse	Hares
Leverets	Partridges
Pheasants	Plovers
Ptarmigan	Quails
Rabbits	Snipe
Teal	Doe Venison
Widgeon	Wild Duck
Woodcock	

VEGETABLES

Jerusalem Artichokes

Aubergines	Broccoli
Brussels Sprouts	
Red Cabbage	Cauliflower
Celeriac	*Celery*
Endive	Horseradish
Parsnips	*Savoys*
Shallots	
Spanish Onions	
Spinach	Watercress

FRUIT

Apricots
Cranberries

Medlars	Melons
Pears	

EMPIRE
IMPORTED
FRESH FRUIT

Apples	Grape Fruit
Oranges	Peaches
Pears	Plums

The following recipes are given during this month:

NOVEMBER RECIPES

Beetroot Soup

Beetroots
Celery
Water
Milk
Cream
Butter

If we cannot afford the time or the expense of preparing an elaborate Russian *Bortsch*, we can try a more modest Beetroot Soup. Bake three beetroots in water for three hours, then peel them and chop them up with a head of celery. Have a pint of water and the same measure of milk in a saucepan, and cook the beetroot and celery in this till they are soft enough to pass through a sieve. Having done this to them, add a spoonful of cream and a little butter, and serve.

Onion Soup

Onions
Butter
Water
Grated cheese

Onion Soup is a great warder-off of colds and chills, and about the easiest in the world to make. Slice half a dozen onions thinly and brown them in butter. Add hot water, salt and plenty of pepper, bring to the boil and continue boiling till the soup is reduced by a quarter. You can eat this either with grated cheese, with small slices of toast on which some cheese has been toasted, or, putting the soup into separate plates add a thin slice or two of French bread dried in the oven, sprinkle with grated cheese and brown quickly in the oven.

Cabbage Soup

Pickled Pork
Cabbage
Bouquet garni
Carrot
Turnip
Parsley
Garlic

Cabbage makes a good winter soup, which has the merit of providing a second course for breakfast as well, for those who like cold pickled pork. Put a pound of pickled pork in a saucepan of cold water with a *bouquet* of parsley, thyme and bayleaf. Cook this for an hour, and then take out the pork and the *bouquet*. Have ready a carrot and a small turnip cut in small pieces, and a good white cabbage finely shredded. Add these to the liquor from the pork with salt and pepper, and cook for another two hours. About half an hour before the soup is wanted, throw in some chopped parsley, a chopped clove of garlic (if you like it), and a little of the pork also cut up fine. This makes a magnificent soup, especially for a family. And you can have the cold pork for breakfast the next morning.

Omelettes come to our tables mostly as 'sweet' or 'savoury', and it is hardly realised what an enormous number of different sorts there are. I do not propose to enter into the question of how to cook an omelette, and in this simple operation each must work out his own salvation. Assuming, however, that there is no difficulty about the cooking, let us note a few ways in which omelettes can be presented to us. In some omelettes the flavour is folded in after the omelette is cooked; in others it is incorporated into the mixture before it is put into the pan. Let us take the 'sweet' omelettes first.

Liqueur Omelettes. The omelette should be seasoned with sugar and a little salt, and cooked in the ordinary way. When it is done, dish it, sprinkle with sugar, pour whatever liqueur you fancy over it, and set it alight on coming to the table. Rum is most commonly met with as an adjunct to omelettes, but other liqueurs are very good.

Jam Omelettes. Season and cook the omelette as above, and when folding put inside it some slightly warm jam. These omelettes can be sprinkled with icing sugar, if liked, and very quickly glazed before serving.

An amusing variant of this jam omelette, which is suitable for Christmas time, is this: Add to the eggs when beating, two tablespoonfuls of cream, a pinch of orange rind and a tablespoonful of rum, these quantities being for six eggs. Fold into the omelette when it is cooked as much warmed mincemeat as it will safely hold, and sprinkle with heated rum, which you will light as the dish is being served.

Marginal notes:
Omelettes

Liqueur
Omelettes

Jam
Omelettes

Christmas
Omelette

Souffléd
Omelettes

Souffléd Omelettes. In this case you beat up the yolks and whites separately. Mix the yolks of three eggs with a quarter of a pound of sugar till smooth, then add by degrees four stiffly-whipped whites. Butter a flat metal or fireproof glass dish and put this mixture on it, giving it the shape of an omelette and seeing that there is some space between it and the edges of the dish to allow for its expansion. Smooth it over and cook in a moderate oven from ten to fifteen minutes, sprinkling it with icing sugar two minutes before you take it out. This omelette can be flavoured with anything you like, the flavouring being added to the yolks before the whites are stirred in.

'Savoury'
Omelettes

Now for the 'Savoury' Omelettes, and first those in which the flavouring is folded in as a sort of stuffing. Here are some 'stuffings':

Asparagus tips tossed in butter.
Artichoke bottoms quartered and tossed in butter.
Chickens' livers tossed in butter.
Soft roes cooked in butter.
Braised endives with cream.
Mushrooms minced and tossed in butter.
Braised lettuce and cream.
Peas *à la française*.
Spinach purée with cream.
Sauté pieces of kidney.
Tomatoes and onions cooked in butter.

A larger number of omelettes are made by mixing the ingredients with the beaten eggs. The omelette is then cooked in the usual way.

Mushrooms minced and tossed in butter.
Very small dice of crust fried in butter.
Very small pieces of lean ham, or tongue.
Fines Herbes, that is, finely chopped parsley, chervil, chives and tarragon.
Half an onion finely minced and cooked in butter, and chopped parsley.
Little *sauté* potato cubes and chopped parsley.
Grated cheese.

Cooked mussels tossed in butter with a little onion and some parsley.

Fried cubes of bacon, spring onions and parsley chopped together, and perhaps a suspicion of garlic.

Pimentoes cut in small pieces and tossed in butter or pork fat. And so on.

This is an omelette named after Arnold Bennett and to be found in the Savoy Grill:

Add a finely chopped fillet of smoked haddock with a little cream to your eggs, add also some pepper, and cook the omelette, but not too much. Do not fold it, but turn it out flat on a dish, coat it with a little Sauce Mornay, sprinkled with grated cheese, and brown quickly.

Smoked Haddock Omelette (Omelette Arnold Bennett)

Eggs
Smoked haddock
Cream
Sauce Mornay
Cheese

This is the Portuguese way of cooking Cod:

Lay two steaks of fresh cod, weighing about half a pound each, in a saucepan where you have already put a good piece of butter, a tablespoonful of olive oil, an onion finely chopped and lightly fried, a tiny piece of bruised garlic, a pinch or two of coarsely chopped parsley, four small peeled, 'de-pipped' and chopped tomatoes, and a *bouquet* of parsley, thyme and bayleaf. Add a good glass of white wine and cook with the lid on over the flame for five minutes. Then take off the lid and complete the cooking at the side of the fire, or on a very low gas, for a quarter of an hour. Arrange the slices on a dish, and pour over them the sauce from which you have removed the *bouquet* at the last moment.

Cod à la Portugaise

Cod
Olive oil
Onion
Garlic
Parsley
Tomatoes
Thyme
Bayleaf
White wine

Cod can very pleasantly be cooked *crème gratin*, for most of us do not share Escoffier's encomiums of this rather uninteresting fish. Boil some cod and divide it into small pieces, skinned and boned, of course. Make a wall of *Duchesse* Potatoes

Cod Crème Gratin

Cod
Duchesse potatoes

Mornay sauce
Parmesan

round a dish, and pour a thin layer of Mornay sauce within it. On this lay the pieces of cod and cover them with more sauce, but not up to the edge of the wall or it will bubble over. Sprinkle grated Parmesan cheese over the sauce, and a little butter, and brown quickly in the oven.

Sole with
Cheese and
Bananas,
'C. M.'

Fillets of sole
Béchamel sauce
Gruyère
Parmesan
Potato purée
Egg
Bananas

A young friend of mine, whose wife was in despair at the sudden arrival of some guests to dinner, told me that she regaled them in the end with the following dish of sole.

Lay some fillets of sole in a buttered dish. Cover them with stock made from the trimmings, and add two or three very small pieces of butter. Poach it gently in the oven. Meanwhile you have cooked a pint of Béchamel sauce with a quarter of a pint of the fish stock. Having let this reduce by half, you have added to it two ounces of grated Gruyère cheese and the same of Parmesan. Now in the dish in which the fillets are to be served, pour a layer of the sauce. Surround this with a wall of potato purée, which you will brush over with beaten egg yolk. Lay the fillets on the sauce and surmount each with a thin long slice of banana previously cooked in a little fresh butter. Pour over a very little more sauce, sprinkle with cheese, and brown the whole quickly in the oven.

Fish Fumet

Onion
Parsley
Fish trimmings
Lemon
White wine
Water

It may be useful here to give a recipe for a really fine Fish Stock or *Fumet*.

Butter the bottom of a stewpan and put in a blanched onion cut in slices, one or two parsley roots or some parsley stalks, and the trimmings and bones of any fish suitable for the purpose. Add the juice of half a lemon, cover the stewpan, leave it on the fire and shake it occasionally. Now add a quarter of a bottle of Chablis, take the lid off and reduce the liquid by fierce boiling to about half. When this is done, add a pint and a half of cold water, bring to the boil, skim and cook for twenty minutes only on a moderate fire.

The use of a *fumet* of this kind will add distinction to any dish.

Sprats require a little care to make them presentable, for we have outgrown the days when we used to fry them on the nursery fire. Here is a recipe which can be applied equally well to sprats or smelts, and to whiting too, though it will take a little longer to cook. Into a well-buttered fireproof dish put two or three tablespoonfuls of Espagnole sauce to which you have added a mixture of a teaspoonful of fried minced onions, some chopped mushroom parings, salt, pepper, nutmeg and chopped parsley. Lay the fish on this bed, surround them with slices of raw mushrooms, add a tablespoonful or two of white wine and cover with more sauce, on which you sprinkle fine browned breadcrumbs. Cook the whole in the oven till it is *gratinée*, that is, browned, and the fish done, and when serving squeeze over a few drops of lemon juice. A little chopped parsley improves its appearance and flavour.

Whiting
Smelts or
Sprats
au gratin

The Fish
Espagnole
sauce
Onions
Mushrooms
Parsley
Lemon
Nutmeg
White wine
Breadcrumbs

Soused Herring and Mackerel are quite familiar to us. Potted Sprats sound, and are, a little more elegant.

Take off the heads and tails, dry them and put them in a fireproof dish. Sprinkle with salt and pepper, and add two bayleaves, a blade of mace, a chopped onion and a little grated nutmeg. Pour over the fish enough vinegar to cover them, add

Potted Sprats

Sprats
Bayleaves
Mace
Onion
Nutmeg
Vinegar

one or two small pats of butter and bake in a moderate oven for twenty minutes or half an hour. Quite a nice cold dish for those who do not dislike vinegar.

Lobster à
l'américaine

Lobster
Oil
Butter
Carrots
Onions
Brandy
White wine
Curry powder
Cayenne
Parsley
Tomato purée

Many are quite passionately devoted to Lobster *à l'américaine*—and rightly, too, I think. It is not a difficult dish to make.

Cook in a saucepan with a tablespoonful of olive oil and a level tablespoonful of butter, two or three carrots and the same number of onions, chopped of course. Cook for five minutes, when you will add the flesh of two or three small lobsters cut in not-too-small pieces. Cook for another five minutes, then throw in a liqueur-glassful of brandy, which you will light and let burn for a few moments. Now add a glassful of white wine, some curry powder and cayenne pepper at your discretion, salt, chopped parsley and a good spoonful of tomato purée. Cover and cook for an hour. A few minutes before serving add a little more brandy and white wine.

Shrimps
Czarina

Shrimps
Béchamel sauce
Cayenne
Mace
Anchovy
essence

For a very simple little dish, try this one.

Make a nice white sauce with butter, flour and three-quarters of a pint of milk, and season it with salt, cayenne, a little mace, and a few drops of anchovy essence. Cook a little and add a pint of picked shrimps. Warm well through, and serve.

Goulash of
Beef

Beef
Lard
Onions
Tomatoes

A goulash of beef, a classic Hungarian dish, is a worthy object of our hungry attention. Cut about three pounds of lean beef into about inch-sized cubes and fry them in a quarter of a pound of lard with half a pound of coarsely chopped onions till the latter are golden. Add a teaspoonful of salt, a pound of peeled and quartered tomatoes, a good teaspoonful of paprika and a wineglassful of water. Cover and cook in the oven for an hour and a half. Now add a teacupful of water and a pound of smallish potatoes cut into fours. Cook in the oven again, stirring now and then, for about an hour or until the liquid has disappeared. This is extraordinarily good for a winter's day, for it is hot in two senses of the word.

Paprika Potatoes

This is rather an unusual way of frying raw minced beef.

Fry a chopped onion in butter, and add a pound of fresh-minced meat and enough stock to moisten it. Take it off the fire, add a little cream, salt and pepper. Shape into rounds and fry them in butter. They should be served on *croûtons* of fried bread, surmounted by a small spoonful of horseradish sauce.

Fried Minced Beef

Onion Raw beef Stock Cream Horseradish sauce

A Mutton Pudding can be made in the same way as a Beefsteak Pudding. Add a little kidney, which will be found to be a great improvement. I fancy some will like the addition of a little onion too.

Mutton Pudding

This is Sausages *en surprise*. Broil some sausages and let them get cold. Make a purée of potato and beat an egg into it. Wrap each sausage, skinned, if you please, in this purée, and egg-and-breadcrumb and fry them. Or you can bake them in the oven, gilding the potato. The long, thin sausages are the best for this, or even the diminutive chipolatas.

Sausages en surprise

Sausages Potato purée Egg Egg and breadcrumbs

Veal cutlets (or *escalopes de veau*) make a useful dish for all occasions. With their various garnishes they have an air of distinction about them which it

Escalopes de veau

is hard for the hostess, or the guests, to resist. May I suggest a few garnishes?

Fried in egg and breadcrumbs and garnished with chopped parsley, hard-boiled egg and anchovy fillets.

With macaroni bound with grated cheese and tomato purée.

With little heaps of freshly-cooked vegetables.

With peas *à la française*.

With a purée of spinach.

With quartered mushrooms tossed in butter.

With various sauces, particularly with a paprika sauce (which, by the way, is delicious with sole).

Kromeskis

Cooked meat
Chicken or veal
Ham or Tongue
Onion
Mushrooms
Béchamel sauce
Egg
Bacon
Batter

Kromeskis are another adornment to a meal, and a very useful way of employing cold meat. Cut up the meat, chicken or veal into very small pieces and mix them with some little bits of ham or tongue, a little onion and some chopped mushrooms tossed in butter, with a little thick Béchamel sauce, so that they are nicely bound together. Add the yolk of an egg, and spread out to cool. When this mixture is cold, shape it into small rolls and wrap each in a very thin rasher of streaky bacon. Dip them in fritter batter and fry them golden. Fish may also be used on occasion to form the stuffing, and the flavouring of the sauce can, of course, be varied.

There are a number of ways of cooking pheasant which are not familiar to us in England, but they are, most of them, too complicated for such simple cookery as is advocated here. It might be worth while remembering, however, that pheasant can be very good when boiled and served with an oyster or celery sauce, while braised pheasant comes within measurable distance of the roast.

Put half a clove of garlic, some powdered herbs and salt and pepper inside the pheasant, which you will now place in a *cocotte* with an ounce and a half of butter. Brown the bird in this, add some good stock, cover the *cocotte* and put it in the oven. Take out the garlic after you have finished your frying, cook the pheasant for three-quarters of an hour, and serve with a purée of chestnuts.

Rabbit is a rather more modest dish than his feathered neighbour, but he makes a very excellent purée.

Bone a young rabbit, pound the flesh and sieve it finely. Season with salt, pepper, a pinch of nutmeg, a little tomato sauce, some good white stock. Put it all in a saucepan and boil it till it is of the same consistency as cream. Eat it with fried *croûtons*. A few small braised onions would do no harm with it.

Stuffed Cabbage is a meat and vegetable course in one.

Boil a large white cabbage in salt water for a quarter of an hour, then take it out, drain it, and open the leaves without breaking them. Now stuff it just plainly between the leaves with sausagemeat or, if you prefer it, a more elaborate farce of veal, bacon, garlic, parsley, thyme, sage and breadcrumbs all bound together with an egg. Close the cabbage up and tie it with string. Put it into a fireproof dish with a good piece of butter, two or three spoonfuls of stock, salt and pepper, and bake it in a moderate oven, basting it well.

Endives, which for some obscure reason are always called chicory in this country, supply a nicely bitter dish when braised. Here is a Belgian way of cooking them. Well butter a flattish saucepan, and lay the endives in it after they have had their outside leaves removed and have been carefully washed. Add a cupful of water, salt and pepper, a few small pieces of butter and a good squeeze of lemon. Cover with a buttered paper and cook them slowly (from half an hour to an hour), turning them once, till they are quite soft but not browned. Thus plain, they can accompany every kind of butcher's meat or, if they are to be served alone, they can be enriched by a Mornay sauce, or served with cream, *hollandaise* or *mousseline* sauces.

Potato Beignets

Potatoes
Cream
Eggs
Frying fat

Potato *beignets* can be served either as an accompaniment to a meat dish or separately as a sweet. Mash some boiled potatoes with an ounce of butter, a pinch of salt (and if they are to be sweet, a little sugar), and a tablespoonful of cream. Mix well till smooth, adding two or more eggs, one by one, till the mixture is stiff enough to be made into little balls, which you can then roll in flour and fry in deep fat, powdering them, if you wish, with a little more sugar. They can be made rather lighter if the yolks are first added and the whites whipped and folded in. In this case no cream should be added.

Duchesse Potatoes

Potatoes
Egg
Nutmeg

Duchesse Potatoes are always exceedingly useful for a garnish.

Mash some potatoes, adding a yolk of egg to every quarter of a pound, and stir to a smooth paste with a little butter. Add salt, pepper and grated nutmeg. Shape the mixture into squares on a floured board, gild them with yolk of egg and bake them in the oven. This mixture is often used for the decoration of dishes by means of a forcing-bag.

NOVEMBER

Potatoes *Duchesse au Chester* are made by simply adding grated cheese to the mixture above.

Potatoes
Duchesse au
Chester

Potatoes *Marquise* are also made from the same mixture, with the addition of a little thick tomato purée. Both these latter are baked in the oven in the same way as the *Duchesse* potatoes.

*Same as above
and Cheese*

Potatoes
Marquise
See Duchesse
*Tomato
Purée*

Last month I recommended cooking apples and flavouring them with Calvados. If you were able to get any of this liqueur, here is another way of using it.

Apples
Flambées
*Apples
Calvados*

Peel and quarter some eating apples, and cook them very carefully in fresh butter in a frying-pan till they are soft and brown on each side. Sprinkle them with castor sugar, pour over a glass of Calvados, set it alight, and serve as the flame dies down.

Orange Fritters can be advantageously *flambées* too.

Orange
Fritters
*Batter
Brandy
Oranges*

Make some pancake batter to which you have added a liqueur-glassful of brandy. Set it aside for two or three hours. Cut the oranges into sections, removing the skin, pips and pith. For each section put two tablespoonfuls of the batter into a cup, put in the section and pour it out with the batter into the frying-pan. Fry for a few minutes and keep it hot.

Now is the exciting moment, which will transform your fritter from the ordinary workaday one. Put all the fritters into a chafing dish (or a pan on the lowest of low flames), pour over a very small glassful of brandy, and set it alight. You may want to add a little sugar, but it is really unnecessary unless you have a very sweet tooth. This is a very delicious dish, and could be used with great effect at a chafing-dish supper, for instance, as the batter would be all the better for keeping.

Peaches Flambées

Peaches Vanilla pod Kirsch or other liqueur

Peaches can, of course, be *flambées* with various liqueurs, Kirsch perhaps being the most popular. Either warm the peach through in the chafing dish or poach it till soft in water with sugar and a vanilla pod. When it is ready, dredge it with a little fine sugar, pour over your Kirsch, or whatever liqueur you have chosen, and set it alight. It is just as well to warm the liqueur slightly, as then it catches fire more quickly; and, if you take my advice, you will have your peach poached.

Peaches with White Wine

Peaches White wine

Here is another way of cooking peaches, which may be served hot or cold. Peel and cut the peaches in half, remove the stones and marinate the fruit for about an hour in a claret-glassful of Sauterne. Now take out the peaches and fry them very lightly in two ounces of butter in a stewpan. Drain them, and make a syrup with sugar of the wine in which they were marinated, adding the kernels to it. When this is ready, pour it over the fruit.

Pancakes, Crêpes Flambées

Pancakes are perhaps more suitable for winter eating than for those spring days in which Shrove Tuesday falls. I have already described one or two superfine ones. Let us now turn our attention to the humbler sort.

It is very seldom that they appear to us in any other shape than a dull roll of batter with a squeeze of lemon juice. Even orange juice is a change. But *crêpes flambées* are a revelation. When the pancakes are made, warm them through again in a pan with a little butter and some crushed sugar rubbed on lemon or orange skin, fold them in four, pour over them whatever liqueur your fancy dictates, set it alight and serve. A little brandy added to the liqueur you choose (provided it has a brandy base) is an improvement, if this dish can be improved.

Sweet pancakes can, of course, be stuffed with jam or with various fruit purées.

Here is a very special pudding, which used to be the delight of my boyhood. It is called Guards' Pudding. Mix well together five ounces of bread-crumbs, three ounces of castor sugar, the same of melted butter, a saltspoonful of carbonate of soda dissolved in a teaspoonful of water, three well-beaten eggs and five tablespoonfuls of raspberry jam. Put it in a buttered mould and steam for a couple of hours. I believe that strawberry jam may be used, but for me the authentic flavour is of raspberries.

Guards'
Pudding

Breadcrumbs
Sugar
Butter
Carbonate of
soda
Eggs
Raspberry or
Strawberry
jam

But just as omelettes can be sweet or savoury, so can pancakes, though this is seldom realised. You can, indeed, stuff them with almost anything, sweet-breads, asparagus tips, peas, caviare (in the Russian manner), or various chopped and seasoned meats. This method of serving them demands, of course, a batter from which the sugar has been omitted. A sauce is often an improvement; for example tomato with the sweetbreads, with the asparagus Béchamel, with perhaps a little grated cheese sprinkled over and browned. There are, in fact, so many ways of presenting pancakes that a Swiss Cookery Book sent to me recently contained forty-six recipes for pan-cakes alone, and it was a little book intended to be by no means comprehensive.

Savoury
Pancakes

IMPORTANT POINTS TO REMEMBER

1. In many of the recipes that follow, *simmering* will be mentioned. Remember that food will simmer just as well in the lower oven as on the simmering (right-hand) hot-plate. To use the lower oven for this purpose not only gives more space on the hot-plate, but, when the hot-plate is not in use, conserves the heat of the stove.

2. It is important to see that the hot-plate lids are always kept down when not in use. Do not keep kettles boiling on the hot-plate. You will only be wasting heat. Remember that the water in the Aga tank is nearly boiling, and will boil up in a minute or two.

3. A wipe in time saves nine. Keep the Aga top clean with a damp cloth as you use it.

DECEMBER

THE FOOD OF THE MONTH

Food which is in season all the year round is given in the table on page 44.

Note.—Newcomers are printed in italics.

FISH

Sea Fish

Bloaters	Cod
Dabs	Gurnet
Haddock	Ling
Skate	Smelts
Sprats	

River Fish

Eels

Shell Fish

Oysters

MEAT

Pork

POULTRY

Ducks	Geese
Turkeys	

GAME

Capercailzie	
Grouse	Hares
Leverets	Partridges
Pheasants	Plovers
Ptarmigan	Quails
Rabbits	Snipe
Teal	Doe Venison
Widgeon	Wild Duck
Woodcock	

VEGETABLES

Jerusalem Artichokes
Broccoli
Brussels Sprouts

Red Cabbage	Celeriac
Celery	Endive
Horseradish	Parsnips
Salsify	Savoys

Shallots
Spanish Onions
Spinach

FRUIT

Apricots
Cranberries

Medlars	Pears

EMPIRE IMPORTED FRESH FRUIT

Apples	Apricots
Grape Fruit	Oranges
Peaches	Pears
Plums	

206

The following recipes are given during this month:

Mushroom
Soup

Mushrooms
Onion
White stock
Flour
Butter
Milk
Cream
and possibly
White wine

Mushroom Soup will be a pleasant luxury in a month when luxuries may occasionally be permitted. Chop up half a pound of fresh mushrooms with a slice of onion. Simmer this in two pints of white stock for twenty minutes, and pass it through a sieve. Thicken this purée with flour and butter, season it well and add a cupful of half milk, half cream. If you like you can add half a wineglassful of Sauterne at the last minute.

Scrambled
Eggs

Scrambled or buttered eggs can be treated, so far as garnishes are concerned, in the same way as eggs *en cocotte* or *sur le plat*.

Scotch
Woodcock

Eggs
Buttered toast
Anchovy paste
Capers
Parsley

One special mixture must not be forgotten, the admirable one which constitutes Scotch Woodcock. Butter the eggs and place them on hot buttered toast spread with anchovy paste. Sprinkle a few chopped capers and a little parsley on each. This makes a lovely savoury, and is often acceptable for breakfast—by the most reluctant.

Scrambled eggs with cheese, with tomatoes, with mushrooms, shrimps, chickens' livers, asparagus tips, flaked smoked fish, little fried crusts . . . all are excellent. And to amuse the children eggs can be emptied out without breaking the shells too much, and the shell filled again with scrambled egg.

Cod à la
créole

Cod
Olive oil
Vinegar
Lemon
Shallot or
Onion

This is a Creole fashion of cooking fresh cod.

Bone the fish and soak it for half an hour, turning it twice or thrice, in a tablespoonful of olive oil, the same of vinegar, a good squeeze of lemon juice and a tablespoonful of chopped shallot or onion. Butter a fireproof dish, put in the fish and pour over it the mixture in which it has been soaked, adding half a pint of tomato purée, a tablespoonful of chopped green pimento (if you have it) and a seasoning of pepper and salt. Cover the dish and bake in a moderate oven for about three-quarters of an hour. When it is done, sprinkle with a little grated cheese and brown.

Tomato purée
Pimento
Cheese

This is a charming manner of cooking a small turbot. Place it in a fireproof dish and pour over it some melted butter. Sprinkle with parsley, thyme and chives finely chopped together, and season with salt and freshly ground black pepper. After it has been left for an hour, brush a beaten egg over it, add some breadcrumbs, and bake in the oven till it is done. Serve with Tartare sauce, from which this method derives its name of Turbot *à la tartare*.

Turbot à la tartare

Turbot
Butter
Parsley
Thyme
Chives
Egg and breadcrumbs
Tartare sauce

Lobster *à la russe* may be very welcome at one of the many meals at Christmas time when cold dishes are in demand. We shall not attempt to aspire to the many operations by which this famous dish is arrived at, but we will cut our cold lobster into slices and coat each with a mixture of mayonnaise sauce and aspic jelly. Having dotted each of these with a little lobster coral, we shall arrange them according to the fancy (or means) of the moment with some *salade russe*, halves of hard-boiled eggs stuffed with caviare, and little rounds of fish jelly surmounted by a piece of truffle.

Lobster à la russe

Lobster
Mayonnaise
Aspic jelly
Salade russe
Hard-boiled eggs
Caviare
Fish jelly
Truffle

Salade russe is very simply made by cutting equal quantities of carrots, potatoes, French beans, peas, capers, gherkins, sliced cooked mushrooms, lobster and lean ham into thin *julienne* strips, adding a few anchovy fillets cut in pieces and binding with a mayonnaise sauce. A garnish of beetroot and caviare may be added.

Salade russe

Potted
Shrimps

Shrimps
Butter
Mace
Cayenne
Nutmeg

Potted shrimps always provide a very delicious stand-by, and they will keep quite well. Into a saucepan in which you have melted three or four ounces of butter put a pint of large shelled shrimps, a blade of mace pounded up, as much cayenne as your palate will bear and, if you care for it, some grated nutmeg. Heat them up slowly and do not let them boil. Pour them into little pots, glasses or *cocottes* (you will serve one to each guest), and cover with melted butter.

Tournedos

Tournedos, which are really the 'kernel' of a fillet of steak, are one of the most popular dishes there are, in witness whereof Escoffier gives nearly seventy ways of presenting them. They are usually grilled, and then served according to the various designations.

Tournedos
Béarnaise

Tournedos *Béarnaise* are one of the most delicious. The tournedos are grilled and served with potatoes cooked in butter and a Béarnaise sauce.

Tournedos à la
niçoise

Tournedos *à la niçoise* are fried tournedos surmounted by half a tablespoonful of chopped tomato, tarragon and a very little garlic tossed in butter, and served surrounded by small separate heaps of French beans and small potatoes.

Tournedos
Rossini

Tournedo *Rossini* are probably not so well known to the palate as the music of their creator to the ear. They are fried in butter and dished upon fried bread. On each is placed a slice of *foie gras* which has been floured and fried in butter: and on each slice of *foie gras* is placed a slice of truffle. They are very rich, but very good indeed.

Mutton
à la bordelaise

Here is another method of using up cold roast

mutton. Toss the pieces of cold mutton in a little butter. In a separate pan cook also in butter two or three shallots (or onions) finely chopped. When these are browning add them to the mutton, as well as a rasher of bacon cut into little pieces, some chopped parsley, salt and pepper. Then pour in a glassful of dry white wine, and simmer for about half an hour.

Cooked mutton
Shallots
or Onions
Bacon
Parsley
White wine

This is something quite different.

Skin some sausages, cut them in half lengthwise and lay half of them in a buttered pie-dish. Sprinkle them with fried sliced onion and slices of raw peeled tomatoes. Season, add the remainder of the sausages, cover with stock and with a thick layer of mashed potatoes. Dot with butter and brown in the oven.

Sausage and Tomato Pie

Sausages
Onions
Tomatoes
Stock
Potatoes

Another simple dish, a *fricassée* of veal (or chicken, of course).

Make a sauce of butter, flour and veal stock, flavoured with pepper, salt and a pinch of nutmeg. Put in some small pieces of cold cooked veal and let it warm through, but do not boil. Add a little cream, stir well again, and just before serving stir in some finely chopped parsley and an egg-yolk beaten with a good squeeze of lemon juice.

Some cooked green peas or mushrooms cut in pieces and tossed in butter may be added, and the *fricassée* may be garnished with small baked tomatoes, rolls of fried bacon or *croûtons* of fried bread.

Fricassée of Veal

Butter
Flour
Veal stock
Nutmeg
Cooked veal
Cream
Parsley
Egg
Lemon

Cold Chicken Legs are usually devilled as a convenient method of disposal. Stuffed and baked legs are more uncommon.

Joint the legs and separate the drumsticks. Marinate them in oil, salt and pepper. Drain them and cover them with the farce described below,

Stuffed Chicken's Legs

Cooked chicken's legs
Oil

Bacon
Farce as below

wrap each in a slice of bacon, tie them up or skewer them and bake them in the oven for about twenty minutes. Dish up on slices of toast.

Farce for
Stuffed
Chicken's
Legs
Breadcrumbs
Lemon
Onion
Sweet herbs
Parsley
Cayenne
Egg

The Farce is composed as follows: two table-spoonfuls of breadcrumbs, half a teaspoonful of finely chopped lemon rind, two slices of onion blanched and finely chopped, half a teaspoonful of chopped sweet herbs, a teaspoonful of chopped parsley seasoned with salt and cayenne pepper and bound with an egg-yolk.

Italian
Turkey
Stuffing
Sausages
Chestnuts
Prunes
Pears
Turkey's liver
White wine
Butter

Here is a most unusual stuffing for the Christmas Turkey. Half cook half a pound of chipolata sausages, let them get cold, skin them and cut them into round slices. Also boil and peel half a pound of chestnuts, and scald half a dozen French prunes which you will then stone and halve. Melt two ounces of butter in a saucepan, and in this cook for a few minutes the pieces of sausage, the chestnuts, the prunes, the skinned and cored quarters of four pears and the turkey's liver blanched and coarsely chopped. Strain off the butter and pour in a glass of white wine, and stuff your turkey with this intriguing mixture.

Ragout of
Turkey,
Goose,
Chicken or
Duck
The remains of
the bird
Onions
Ham or bacon
Tomatoes
Bouquet garni
Beef stock
Goose or bacon
fat

Goose we should have some time at Christmas-tide, if only to eat up his remains in a masterly stew which hails from that part of France where goose is understood! Brown the pieces in goose fat and, having taken them out, cook in the same fat a couple of thinly sliced onions and a slice of raw ham or bacon cut in small dice. Skin four tomatoes and remove the pips, cut them up and add them, with a *bouquet* of parsley, thyme and bayleaf, to the onion and ham. Pour in three cupfuls of beef stock, or water, liberally seasoned with pepper and some salt, bring

DECEMBER

to the boil and cook for a quarter of an hour. Now remove the *bouquet*, and simmer for two hours. The remains of turkey, chicken or duck can be disposed of in the same way, and if you have no goose fat, then bacon fat is permissible, though not quite so good.

Cold Turkey demands a Cranberry Sauce. Dissolve enough sugar in water to make a thickish syrup, boil it for ten minutes and then add half a pint of cranberries. Put on the lid and cook very gently (so that the berries do not burst) till they are tender and transparent, skimming now and then. This sauce is better if you make it the day before you want to use it.

Cranberry Sauce (Cold)

Cranberries Sugar

One last Pudding, this time of Rabbit. Keep back the head, neck, liver and kidneys; cut the rest of the rabbit into neat pieces. Rub the pieces with a mixture of flour, salt and pepper, and put them in the paste-lined pudding-basin interspersed with cubes of pickled pork, and proceed as usual. Send to the table with gravy made from the head and other parts.

Rabbit Pudding

Rabbit Pickled pork Suet paste

Potato *croquettes* are made from the same kind of purée as is required for *Duchesse* potatoes. Make little balls of the mixture, roll them in flour, egg-and-breadcrumb them and fry them in deep fat. They can also be varied by the addition of cheese or tomato purée to the purée, and make an admirable accompaniment to numerous entrées.

Potato Croquettes

Potato purée Egg and breadcrumbs Frying fat and possibly Cheese

Potatoes are always a little difficulty at a time when the menu requires careful supervision, as at Christmas time. It is perfectly easy to vary them without undue trouble, and often almost the same dish

213

varied a little in its manner of presentation will give an impression of something entirely different.

Potatoes
Chatouillard

For instance, the ordinary method of frying raw potatoes in this country comprises only the two varieties known as 'fried' and 'chips'. Straw potatoes —that is, cut into the thinnest of thin strips and fried —are a pleasing change, especially with game. *Soufflées* potatoes we have already noted. Potatoes cut into long ribbons of the same thickness can also be treated in the same way, and are called *Pommes de Terre Chatouillard*.

Potatoes
Noisettes

Potatoes
Château

Potatoes
Pont-Neuf

Quite a different way of frying potatoes is to shape them into pieces the size of hazel-nuts (*Noisettes*), of a large olive (*Château*), or into half-inch cubes (*Pont-Neuf*). Sprinkle them with salt and pepper, and cook them gently in butter till they are soft and golden. Serve with chopped parsley scattered over them.

Fried Celery

Celery
Lemon
Egg and
breadcrumbs
or Batter

While we are on the subject of frying, do not let us forget our friend Celery. Cut it into pieces, cross-wise, about three inches in length. Cook them till tender in boiling water with a little lemon juice. Drain and dry well. Egg-and-breadcrumb them or dip them in batter, and then fry them. Mostly this is to be used as a garnish to grills, but fried or grilled bacon and fried celery makes a good luncheon or impromptu supper dish.

Stuffed
Tomatoes

Tomatoes
Peas or
Egg
Cheese
Breadcrumbs

Four months ago we discussed the question of stuffed tomatoes. The weather then demanded that they should be cold. We might very well consider what we can do with them when hot.

The simplest way is to scoop them out and fill them with new peas (tinned) plainly boiled or cooked *à la française*. Or fill them with beaten egg, grated cheese and just enough breadcrumbs to stop the mixture from getting wet, and bake in the oven.

Tomatoes
stuffed à la
napolitaine
*Tomatoes
Butter
Flour
Cheese
Milk*

Here is the Neapolitan way. Cut the tomatoes in half, remove the cores and pips, salt and pepper them. Now make a thick sauce with butter, flour, grated cheese and a little milk. Fill the tomatoes with this and bake for half an hour.

Tomatoes
stuffed with
Eggs
*Tomatoes
Eggs
Cheese
Breadcrumbs*

Tomatoes can be stuffed with eggs, by cutting off a piece of the top of the tomatoes, scooping out the core and pulp and breaking into each a whole egg. Sprinkle with grated cheese, browned breadcrumbs and a little melted butter, and cook in the oven till the egg is set.

Tomatoes
stuffed with
Meat
*Tomatoes
Oil or Butter
Breadcrumbs
Milk
Onion
Cold meat*

For a change stuff them with any meat you have over. Cut some large ripe tomatoes in half and scoop out the cores and juice. Put them aside and make a stuffing by cooking gently with a little oil or butter the insides of the tomatoes, salted and peppered, a few fine breadcrumbs soaked in milk, a small onion finely chopped and some cold meat also chopped small. When this is nearly done, put the tomatoes in the oven for a quarter of an hour, then take them out and stuff them with the mixture. Pile it well up in them, sprinkle with browned breadcrumbs and melted butter, and brown in the oven.

Tomatoes
stuffed à la
portugaise
*Tomatoes
Rice
Parsley*

The Portuguese stuff them with some pilaff rice mixed with chopped tomato, and serve them sprinkled with parsley.

The Provençal fashion is a trifle more complicated, but very savoury. Cut half a dozen tomatoes in half, scoop out their insides and cook the cases in oil, cut side down, till half cooked, then turn them over and cook a little longer. Meanwhile

provençale

Tomatoes
Oil
Onion
Parsley
Garlic
Breadcrumbs
Stock
Anchovies
Cheese

fry two tablespoonfuls of chopped onion in oil, then add four peeled and roughly chopped tomatoes, a pinch of chopped parsley and a crushed clove or garlic, cover and cook for ten minutes. Now add four tablespoonfuls of breadcrumbs soaked in stock, and two pounded anchovies. Stuff the tomatoes, which you have removed to the serving dish, with this mixture, sprinkle them with grated cheese, breadcrumbs and a little oil, and finish in the oven. These tomatoes may be served hot or cold.

Chocolate
Soufflé

Chocolate
Milk
Butter
Flour
Vanilla essence
Sugar
Eggs

A cold Chocolate *Soufflé* can be made in the same way as the Orange *Soufflé* mentioned in June, but just now many will prefer a hot one.

Simmer two ounces of finely grated chocolate with half a pint of milk till the former is dissolved, then add it to an ounce of melted butter with which has been mixed three ounces of flour. Boil this well, let it cool a little and add half a teaspoonful of vanilla essence, two ounces of sugar and the yolks of three eggs one by one. Stir and beat up well, then add lightly the whipped-up whites of three eggs. Turn into a *soufflé* dish and cook for about three-quarters of an hour.

Chestnut
Cake

Chestnuts
Sugar
Vanilla
Almonds
Preserved
fruit

A jolly Chestnut Cake, which is strongly reminiscent of *marrons glacés*, can be made by first boiling two pounds of chestnuts till they are soft, then skinning them and passing them through a sieve. Add to the ensuing purée a thick syrup made with a pound of sugar flavoured with vanilla, and stir it all together till it is a thick paste. By the way, you should put a little of the syrup aside. Now shape the paste on the dish on which it is to be served, decorate it with almonds and preserved fruit, and glacé it with the rest of the syrup about two hours before you want to eat it.

Another stand-by, this time a sweet, are *petits pots de crème*, an invention, I believe, of the eighteenth century. Fill eight little pots with milk, and put it all into a saucepan with three ounces of sugar and the flavouring you have chosen. Boil it up and let it get cold. Now beat up the yolks of six eggs (your potted ones will do at a pinch), add them to the milk and pass through a hair sieve. With this fill the pots and cook them in the oven in a baking-dish of water till they are set, which will take about twenty minutes. They are, of course, served cold, and it is difficult to persuade your guests that they are not made with cream. Almost any flavour can be used, vanilla, coffee, chocolate, lemon, orange, even tea. They can also be made with plain black coffee instead of milk, but they may be a little watery this way.

Petits pots de crème

Milk
Eggs
Sugar
Flavouring

Marrons glacés give a touch of distinction to any dessert, and, though they are expensive to buy, they can be made quite simply as follows. Peel and boil as many chestnuts as you will want. Clarify some sugar and boil the chestnuts in it for a few minutes. Then coat them thickly with sugar, brown them in the oven and at the last minute squeeze a few drops of lemon juice over them.

If you have made the *pots de crème*, your egg whites will come in useful for making méringues, the easiest thing in the world. Do not forget that their cream filling can be improved by the addition of a flavouring. Cherry jam makes a particularly delicious one.

Marrons Glacés

Chestnuts
Sugar
Lemon

Meringues à la
suisse

Meringues
Chocolate
Cream
Almonds

A Swiss manner of serving them is good and picturesque. Make the méringues of different sizes and put a layer at the bottom of a dish. Pour over a mixture of melted chocolate and whipped cream, then another layer of méringues, and so on till the dish is full. On the last layer of cream and chocolate sprinkle a good dusting of chopped roasted almonds.

Cheese Tart

Pastry
Gruyère cheese
Egg
Cream

This is a real Cheese Tart, not a Lemon Cheese one.

Make some pastry and put it in a *flan* mould. Cook it for about twenty minutes. Then fill it with a well-beaten mixture of a quarter of a pound of grated Gruyère cheese, an egg and a good cupful of cream. Cook for a quarter of an hour longer, when the contents of the tart should be an exquisite gold colour.

There are various ways of making a Risotto, and many have become quite lyrical about this dish. We will satisfy ourselves with a recipe from Piedmont. Fry a medium-sized onion, finely chopped, in butter, and add to it half a pound of uncooked Carolina rice. In my opinion, this should not be washed first, but simply shaken to remove any dust. If your scruples allow you to follow my example, I advise you to do so. Now put the pan on a very low heat, add a pinch or two of saffron, and let the rice get thoroughly saturated with the butter. Now add a cupful of *consommé*, or good stock, cover the rice and let it cook very slowly till the stock is absorbed. Then add a little more stock, letting that be absorbed in its turn, until you have added in all about a pint of stock for this quantity of rice. Stir with a wooden spoon when the stock is being added, and as a result of your loving care you should have in the end a compact creamy mass of rice, in which, however, each grain of rice preserves its 'identity' and does not help to compose the sloppy agglomeration which usually passes muster for this Italian dish. Add at the last a few pieces of fresh butter and some grated Parmesan, which you stir in, as well as a few small dice of lean cooked ham.

According to another writer, a Milanese Risotto is made in the same manner, save that a little wine and tomato purée should be added before the stock is put in, and that the risotto can be made 'more opulent' (a good touch, that!) with mushrooms and truffles.

Risotto à la milanaise

A NOTE ON
SAUCES

★

In this chapter I have written down a few sauces of the kind that those who like good food will appreciate and may wish to have by them, for easy reference. Some are mentioned in the body of the book; others are not, but they will all be found good and useful. In the following recipes I have not been guided by simplicity or economy, because a really good sauce is always worth making properly (though the ingenious may be able to find a few short cuts which will still allow the sauce to retain something of its authentic flavour), and if the time and ingredients for its preparation cannot be spared, it is often better to leave it out or to employ a simpler one more suited to the occasion. Neither have I given any sauces for sweets, for these can easily be found in any good cookery book, and, strictly speaking, I suppose they are hardly sauces in the true sense of the word, but more usually syrups or purées.

Sabayon occurs to my mind, however, as a more important sauce for sweets, so perhaps I should give it here.   Sabayon

For a small sauce mix a quarter of a pound of powdered sugar with three egg yolks in a basin. Add half a pint of dry white wine, and whisk it in a pan set in boiling water till it is firm and frothy and about four times its original size. It can be made with milk instead of wine, if desired, and can then be flavoured according to your liking.

SAUCES

It should always be remembered that sauces need careful cooking. They must be smooth and light, and their correct seasoning ascertained by frequent tasting. They cannot be thrown together in a moment, and, needless to say, they should never be lumpy. If they are stirred as they should be, and not cooked too fast, they should be quite free from this intolerable blemish (which, by the way, is equally a crime in potato purée), but straining will always make certain that lumps are absent.

Experience only can tell how the best results can be obtained with the commodities at one's command, and a little adventuring will do no harm. Above all, a sauce should never be so strongly flavoured as to kill the taste of the dish it accompanies, and a proper manipulation of the dish's various ingredients will ensure that the sauce not only sets off the food to its best advantage, but will itself be given its proper value in the meal.

★　　★　　★

Directions for making the following Sauces are given in this book.

SAUCES

★   ★   ★

Roux

There are a few sauces which may be called 'basic' sauces and will be mentioned in this chapter as ingredients in others. I will give these first. The others will follow in alphabetical order. I assume that my readers are familiar with the word ' *roux*', which denotes the mixture of flour and butter that constitutes the thickening agent. White *roux* is the flour mixed with the butter and not cooked at all before the liquid is introduced, or only for a long enough time to dissipate the disagreeable taste of raw flour. Pale *roux* is cooked until just before the colour begins to change. Brown *roux* until the flour has acquired a light brown colour and smells slightly nutty. (Slow cooking is of the utmost importance here.)

I also assume that the method of preparing Stock is understood, as the ultimate flavour of the sauce depends so much upon the flavour which the stock adds to it.

Espagnole or Brown Sauce

Espagnole or Brown Sauce is much used in the preparation of others. This is a simple way of making it.

Put three carrots and one onion, all cut up, into a pan with some butter and some scraps of meat, game or veal. Cover and cook slowly till the onions are a pale brown, then add a tablespoonful of flour, brown that slightly, too, and then add enough stock to get the required moisture. Stir till it thickens, add a *bouquet* of parsley, thyme and bay, and simmer gently for about an hour. Season and strain. This sauce will keep in ordinary weather for several days if it is stored in a covered jar.

Half-Glaze

Take a quart, or a lesser quantity, of Espagnole Sauce and cook it with an equal quantity of brown stock till it is reduced—in the case of two quarts—to nine-tenths of a quart. Strain and finish off the fire with a tenth of a quart of sherry.

Velouté

This sauce is made by adding White Stock to a pale *roux*. A few mushroom parings may be added, if liked, but the flavour of the stock should really be sufficient. Fish *Velouté* is, of course, made with fish stock.

Allemande Sauce

This is really a thickened *velouté*, and is made by mixing a pint of *velouté* with half a pint of cold white stock, the yolks of two eggs, a good squeeze of lemon juice and a little mushroom liquor. Stir this till it is reduced by about a third and add a little cream.

This is the familiar White Sauce made with a white *roux* and boiling milk. The perfect Béchamel is achieved by boiling the milk with an onion stuck with cloves, a little grated nutmeg, salt, pepper and thyme. It should cook slowly for about an hour, but many of us will hardly find the time for this perfection, and a perfectly good one can be made in half the time.

Béchamel Sauce

One. Quarter four tomatoes and put them in a saucepan with a carrot and an onion finely chopped, salt and pepper, and, if you like, a pinch of basil. Cover with water, bring to the boil and cook well. Sieve it, add brown *roux*, a little good stock, and reduce till fairly thick.

Tomato Sauce, I

Two. Make a brown *roux* and add to it some tinned tomato purée, a very little stock, a small piece of butter, salt, pepper and a grating of nutmeg. Simmer for ten minutes or so. (This is if you want to make the sauce in a hurry.)

Tomato Sauce, II

Reduce a couple of tablespoonfuls of vinegar, to which you have added a little pepper, till there is half the quantity, and pour into this the yolks of three eggs, salt, and a nice piece of butter which you have previously mixed in a basin. Stir all together over the fire in a pan of boiling water, adding small pieces of butter till it is smooth. It must be served at once.

Hollandaise Sauce

Here are a few other sauces of a kind which may be found useful with the various dishes I have mentioned.

Béarnaise Sauce

Cook in a saucepan two shallots (or onions) finely chopped, a little chopped tarragon (or a dash of tarragon vinegar) and a glass of white wine, till it is reduced by a third. Mix the yolks of three eggs with a small piece of butter and a little cayenne pepper, and pour the liquid over them. Sieve, and cook gently in another saucepan till it thickens, taking care not to boil it. Before serving, sprinkle in a very little lemon juice and some chopped parsley. It should be fairly stiff, and is excellent with *tournedos*, for example.

Bercy Sauce

Cook some chopped shallots (or onions) in butter without browning them and moisten them with half white wine and half *velouté* made with fish stock. Reduce and add chopped parsley before serving.

Bordelaise Sauce

This is a simple method. Cook quickly in oil for five minutes two shallots, a small onion and three or four mushrooms all chopped up. Then add a little flour, a tablespoonful of stock, the same of tomato purée, salt, pepper and chopped parsley. This should then be reduced by a quarter and served at once.

Chasseur Sauce

This sauce is rather complicated and expensive, but as we have often enjoyed it, we might as well know how to make it.

Fry half a dozen minced mushrooms in a level dessertspoonful of butter and the same of oil. When they are slightly browned add a small teaspoonful of minced shallots (or onions). Drain off half the fat and add half a pint of white wine and a liqueur-glassful of brandy. Reduce by half, and finish with half a pint of half-glaze, half that quantity of tomato sauce and a tablespoonful of melted meat glaze. Boil for five minutes longer, and just before serving sprinkle in some chopped parsley.

SAUCES

Reduce a pint of half-glaze by about a third, adding while it is reducing about three-quarters of a pint of meat jelly by degrees. Season and add, off the fire, a little Madeira or Port. Stir while it cools, until it is of the right consistency to coat whatever you are preparing.

Chaud-Froid Sauce (Brown)

A White Chaud-Froid Sauce is made by reducing in the same way a pint of *velouté* to which you have added three-quarters of a pint of chicken or veal jelly, and gradually adding half a pint of cream.

Chaud-Froid Sauce (White)

You can colour this sauce with tomato purée, or if you want a more delicate shade and flavour, with paprika, this variant being known as *Chaud-Froid à l'Aurore*.

Chaud-Froid Sauce à l'Aurore

This is a Béarnaise Sauce tinted and flavoured with a purée of tomatoes.

Choron Sauce

This sauce has already been described on page 213.

Cranberry Sauce

An admirable cold sauce can be made as follows. Dissolve four tablespoonfuls of red-currant jelly, and add a good glass of port, a teaspoonful of finely chopped and blanched shallots, the same of orange rind cut in *julienne* strips and blanched, the same of lemon rind similarly treated, a teaspoonful of mustard, a little cayenne pepper and powdered ginger, the juice of an orange and the juice of half a lemon. Mix all well together. It is particularly good with cold venison, and with cold mutton, too.

Cumberland Sauce

Fry in a little butter a small onion, two shallots and a little bacon chopped together. Pour in a glass of white wine, a little vinegar, and add a *bouquet* of thyme, parsley and bay. Reduce by a quarter and

Devil Sauce

enrich by the addition of a little white stock and a little tomato purée, and season with salt, pepper and cayenne. Boil for about five minutes and strain. Piquancy can be given by the addition of Harvey Sauce or Escoffier Sauce at the end.

Hungarian Sauce

Fry in butter, without browning them, two table-spoonfuls of chopped onion, seasoned with salt and plenty of paprika. Add a quarter of a pint of white wine and a *bouquet*, reduce by two-thirds and remove the *bouquet*, add a pint of *velouté*, and boil for five minutes. Strain carefully, and before serving add a good piece of butter. This sauce, especially with veal cutlets, will taste even nicer than it looks.

Indienne Sauce

Though Béchamel Sauce flavoured with curry powder often does service for this sauce, the following gives the more authentic flavour, in which the curry should not be too pronounced. Cook a piece of butter the size of a small egg with a tablespoonful of flour till it is well cooked but not brown. Add a good pinch of saffron and of curry powder, and stir and cook a little more. Then add by degrees a large cupful of milk, and season with salt, pepper and grated nutmeg. More milk can be added if it is too thick, or more seasoning if necessary. Make it creamy at the last moment with a little more butter.

Lyonnaise Sauce

Mince enough onion to make two or three table-spoonfuls, and brown them lightly in two ounces of butter. Add a quarter of a pint of white wine, and the same of vinegar, and reduce till the liquid has almost disappeared. Now add a pint and a half of half-glaze and cook for half an hour. The little pieces of onion may be left in, or the sauce may be strained, as you like.

SAUCES

Melt a largish piece of butter with a coffeespoonful of water and the juice of a lemon. Warm well, add salt and at the last minute some chopped parsley.

Add to a Béchamel Sauce as much grated Gruyère and Parmesan cheese as your palate demands (or Cheddar cheese will do at a pinch). Some add the beaten yolk of an egg, but this is really unnecessary. A touch of cayenne pepper, or paprika, often improves it.

Put into a saucepan the yolks of two eggs, a drop of cold water, salt, pepper and the juice of a quarter of a lemon. Stand the saucepan in a pan of boiling water, and add one by one small pieces of butter, stirring all the time as you would in making a Mayonnaise Sauce. Do not let it get too hot, and go on adding the butter till the sauce is soft and creamy. Do not be upset if the first attempt is a failure, but try again. It is as temperamental as mayonnaise—and as easy to make when once you have the knack.

Mustard Sauce can be made either by adding mustard to a Hollandaise Sauce, or as follows. Make a butter sauce with half an ounce of butter, the same of flour and half a pint of boiling water. When this is mixed, but not boiling, add the yolks of two eggs, a little cream and the juice of half a lemon. Finish with more butter and about a dessertspoonful of mustard.

A third way is to stir a dessertspoonful of flour into an ounce of melted butter, adding salt, pepper, a tablespoonful of dry mustard, a teaspoonful of

SAUCES

vinegar and a little water. Stir on a slow heat till it thickens, and thank God for it and fine fresh herrings!

Orange Sauce

Cut the rind of an orange into thin *julienne* strips, and cook them for five minutes in boiling water. Drain them and add to them a cupful of Espagnole Sauce, pepper, salt and the juice of two oranges and one lemon. Stir till very hot.

Paprika Sauce

This is the same as the Hungarian Sauce already described.

Piquante Sauce

Put two chopped shallots into a saucepan with a *bouquet* and three tablespoonfuls of vinegar (or fifty-fifty white wine and vinegar). Reduce it to a third, and add some stock or gravy. Mix in a brown *roux*, cook a little longer and, when you have seasoned it to your liking, add some chopped gherkins, capers and parsley and freshly ground black pepper.

Portuguese Sauce

Fry some chopped onion lightly in oil. Add some coarsely chopped peeled tomatoes, salt, freshly ground pepper, tomato sauce, a little garlic, chopped parsley and a little meat glaze.

Provençale Sauce

Fry some coarsely chopped tomatoes in smoking oil. Then add salt, pepper, a pinch of sugar, a little chopped parsley and a small piece of garlic. Cook for twenty minutes, having added some chopped mushrooms tossed in oil. Strain and finish with a tomato sauce.

Ravigote Sauce

Boil a quarter of a pint of white wine with half that amount of vinegar till it is reduced by half. Add a pint of *velouté*, boil for a few minutes and add finally some pressed shallots pounded with butter,

SAUCES

and a sprinkling of chopped chervil, tarragon and chives.

A cold Ravigote Sauce is made by mixing the following well together:—oil, vinegar, salt, pepper, and chopped onions, capers, parsley, chervil and tarragon.

Red Sauce

A curious sauce, well worth trying, which is used in Spain for cooking fish, is made by pounding together a little garlic and a couple of parboiled, skinned and 'de-pipped' pimentoes. Add a large cupful of water, and mix. This mixture must be added, with a little salt and a drop or two of vinegar, to a cupful of oil which you have brought to the boil in a saucepan. After you have cooked the fish in this, let the sauce reduce, and strain it.

Robert Sauce

Fry in butter a large minced onion without browning it. Add a third of a pint of white wine, reduce this by a third, then add a pint of half-glaze, and simmer for twenty minutes. At the last add a tablespoonful of meat glaze, a pinch of sugar and a teaspoonful of mustard. Do not let it boil again. (You can get a Robert Sauce in the Escoffier products, which only requires the addition of some brown stock to make an excellent hot sauce.)

Saffron Sauce

Saffron is little used generally in this country outside Cornwall, where the baker's windowful of yellow saffron buns is always a mysterious sight to the stranger. However, if any of us have carried away a taste for saffron, this simple sauce may sometimes be used. Simply add to a Béchamel Sauce a pinch of saffron to your taste, and cook it for twenty minutes or so.

Soubise Sauce

This is a more distinguished relative of our homely onion sauce. Fry some minced onions with-

231

out colouring them, and add some Béchamel Sauce.
Cook for half an hour, and season to taste.

This sauce can be made even more distinguished
by the addition of tomato purée or paprika.

Vinaigrette Sauce

This sauce, which is so pleasant with cold asparagus, is the same as cold Ravigote Sauce, for which
see above.

Vin Blanc Sauce

This is a simple, but somewhat unorthodox way
of making a White Wine Sauce. Simply make a
brown *roux*, add a glassful of white wine and boil
for a few minutes. Many cooks will hardly agree
with this, but it is quite a good substitute for the
real thing, which is rather complicated to make.
Sole *au vin blanc* should be attempted by all.

There are one or two variations of Mayonnaise
Sauce, which I should like to mention.

Andalusian Sauce

Finish a Mayonnaise Sauce with a purée of
tomatoes, and add to it small dice of red pimentoes.

Bohemian Sauce

This is a kind of mayonnaise made by mixing
some cold Béchamel Sauce, which has been made
with the addition of the yolks of eggs, with salt,
pepper and vinegar. Add oil in the same way as
for Mayonnaise Sauce, and thin it with tarragon
vinegar.

Chantilly Sauce

This is an ordinary Mayonnaise Sauce which has
been thinned down with lemon juice instead of
vinegar. Just before serving, some whipped cream
should be folded into it.

Italian Sauce

A Mayonnaise Sauce made with lemon juice, to
which chopped cooked brains and parsley have been
added.

SAUCES

A purée of apples cooked in white wine mixed with Mayonnaise Sauce and some grated horseradish.

Swedish Sauce

Grated horseradish can be added to a plain mayonnaise with very happy results.

Au Raifort

This is a Mayonnaise Sauce flavoured with mustard. Chopped capers, parsley, gherkins, chervil and tarragon should be added to it, and finally a drop or two of anchovy essence.

Remoulade Sauce

It is sometimes more decorative to have another colour than yellow for one's mayonnaise. It can be turned red by a little pounded flesh of red pimentoes, if it is wanted for meat; or if for fish, then the pounded coral of a hen lobster will do equally well.

Red Mayonnaise Sauce

The simplest way of turning it green is to boil a little spinach, parsley, watercress and chervil for six or seven minutes, squeeze to a pulp, and use the liquid as your colouring agent.

Green Mayonnaise Sauce

Tartare Sauce is a Mayonnaise Sauce strongly seasoned and with chopped onions and chives added to it. Another version adds mustard and parsley, gherkins, capers and tarragon chopped together.

Tartare Sauce

And lastly, there are one or two butters. Black Butter (*Beurre noir*) has been described on page 163. Brown Butter (*Beurre noisette*) is the same, only it is not browned so much.

Brown Butter (Beurre noisette)

White Butter (*Beurre blanc*) is made by putting two finely chopped shallots into a saucepan and adding salt, freshly ground pepper, and a couple of tablespoonfuls of vinegar. Cook a little and then put in, one by one, five pieces of butter the size of

White Butter (Beurre blanc)

233

SAUCES

a large nut. Stir with a wooden spoon for a few minutes, but see that it does not boil.

Finally, there are the butters for garnishing, or finishing sauces. I will give one or two of the more common ones.

Shrimp Butter
Mix pounded shrimps with their own weight in butter. Strain well and cool.

Lobster Butter
Mix the spawn and creamy parts of a lobster, well pounded together, with their weight in butter, and proceed as before.

Maître d'hôtel Butter
Soften your butter and add to it, for each half-pound, a tablespoonful of chopped parsley, salt, pepper and a few drops of lemon juice.

Other butters, which can be used in garnishing *hors d'œuvres* or for filling hard-boiled eggs, can be made by pounding with good butter such ingredients as Caviare, Curry Powder, Fillets of Red Herrings, Horseradish, Smoked Salmon, Paprika, Pimento, Game, Tunny Fish, and so on. These 'butters' can be enriched with cream.

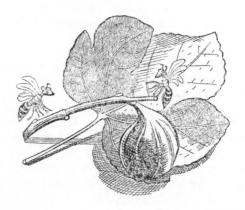

INDEX TO PART TWO

NOTE: *The index to the methods of using the* AGA *will be found on page* 41.

INDEX

INDEX

INDEX

INDEX

INDEX

INDEX

INDEX

INDEX

If you have enjoyed this Persephone book why not telephone or write to us for a free copy of the Persephone Catalogue and the current Persephone Quarterly? All Persephone books ordered from us cost £10 or three for £27 plus £1 postage per book.

PERSEPHONE BOOKS LTD
59 Lamb's Conduit Street
London WC1N 3NB

Telephone: 020 7242 9292
Fax: 020 7242 9272
sales@persephonebooks.co.uk
www.persephonebooks.co.uk

Persephone Books publishes forgotten fiction and non-fiction by unjustly neglected authors. The following titles are available: